GRIEF RELIEF

IN 30 MINUTES

AURORA WINTER

Get your bonuses! Visit:

www.GetCoachTraining.com
Get 5 free coach training videos—learn coaching tools to help yourself and help others. You will learn bonus coaching skills that are not covered in this book.

Learn what to say—and not say—to encourage others. Learn how to see at a glance if your life is off-balance—and what to do about it. Learn how to double your happiness and peaceful productivity. Learn the 5 secrets of successful coaches, and more!
(Over $100 value—yours free for a limited time.)

www.AuroraWinter.com
Get Aurora to speak at your next event. Serious inquires only, please: 866-344-3108 or Aurora@AuroraWinter.com

www.GriefCoachAcademy.com
Interested in a career helping others? Learn how you can make a difference. Find out about our upcoming teleseminars and events. Books, audio books, CDs, home study training, articles, TV interviews, and more resources online.

PRAISE

"I admire Aurora and her work because she is living the sermon and has turned a curse into a blessing by helping others heal. Others can gain strength from her wisdom and experience."
—Dr. Bernie Siegel, author *Love, Medicine, and Miracles*

"I've gone from minus 10 to plus 10…in 10 minutes. The Peace Method® is amazing! Everyone should try it. "
—Leslie Singer, coach

"The Peace Method® in this book is a gift sent straight from heaven…it's amazingly simple and effective for reframing grief and revealing a whole world of inspiring possibilities."
—Kelly Sullivan Walden, best-selling author *I Had the Strangest Dream*

"After a 20 minute process doing the Peace Method® with Aurora, my life has changed. It's amazing, incredible, indescribable! I have joy in my heart that I have not had for 4 ½ years. I recommend Aurora—her content, her heart, her mentorship."
—Miki Knowles, young widow, coach

"I have coached many people using this simple five-step process, and it is my favorite coaching tool. It is amazing how quickly my clients shift to peace, happiness, and empowerment with the Peace Method®."
—Babette Zschiegner, certified *From Heartbreak to Happiness®* coach, author *Traveling with your Autistic Child*

"Aurora offers wise tools for appreciating the everyday beauty of living."
—Rev. Dr. Michael Beckwith, author *Spiritual Liberation*, featured in the hit movie *The Secret*

"Aurora inspires us to find the healing in the pain, the gift in the grief, the love on the other side of sadness."
—Paul Ferrini, author *Reflections of the Christ Mind*

"Aurora helped me release my grief the day after a beloved family member died. I experienced a profound shift from pain to peace in less than 30 minutes. The Peace Method® works--try it!
—Ann Raisch, master certified From Heartbreak to Happiness® coach

"Aurora is very comforting and reassuring. She's upbeat while giving nuggets of information that are useful, helpful and practical. I recommend her as a guest—and as a writer."
—Jenny Toste, host ABC-TV

"Thank you for sharing, Aurora. You created a mind-shift within me and brought me greater peace about my divorce. Thanks for helping me—and my audience, too."
—Jordana Green, WCCO radio host

"If anyone knows how to turn misery into miracles, it's Aurora Winter. She is a leading coach and thought leader in the world today."
— Dr. Pat Baccili, radio host

GRIEF RELIEF

IN 30 MINUTES

How to use the

Peace Method®

to go from heartbreak to happiness

❧

Aurora Winter

AURORA WINTER

Published by Same Page LLC 12021 Wilshire Boulevard, Los Angeles, CA 90025

Cover design by Yale Winter

ISBN 978-0-9722497-5-1

DEDICATION

*Dedicated to all the students at the
Grief Coach Academy, and our work
to revolutionize the way that
people heal from grief.*

Table of Contents

INTRODUCTION

BUSTING THE MYTH "IT JUST TAKES TIME"

When I was grieving, well-meaning people who sincerely cared about me told me, "It just takes time."

And so I waited ... and waited ... and waited. Time passed — but it did not heal my grief.

"It just takes time" is a tragic myth. It is a self-fulfilling prophesy.

Grief can knock people lastingly below their former happiness level. In his extensive research on adaptation, psychologist Dr. Edward Diener discovered two life events that devastate happiness for years: loss of a spouse and loss of a job. It typically takes five to eight years for a widow to regain her former sense of well-being, as reported in TIME magazine on January 17, 2005.

Five to eight years is too long! It's not the grieving person's fault. They simply haven't been taught what to do, or how to release their grief more quickly.

The cost of suffering from grief is staggering. Joy, health, vitality, relationships, creativity, productivity, clarity and prosperity all suffer. The Wall Street Journal reported that the workplace cost of grief is $75 billion per year in the US due to lost productivity, accidents, and absenteeism. Chronic stress from grief can prematurely age your cells by a decade. It can even trigger death.

Knowing that millions of people suffer from grief for years, as I did, drove me to find a solution. It inspired me to devote 20 years to studying happiness and grief recovery. It motivated me to found the Grief Coach Academy. It compelled me to create a coaching recipe to accelerate the healing process. I don't want people to suffer one minute longer than necessary.

Happiness is an inside job. Life circumstances do not determine your happiness — you do. Dr. David Lykken from the University of Minnesota studied 4,000 sets of identical twins over two decades. He came to the conclusion that less than 10% of happiness is due to life circumstances. A hefty 40% of your happiness is under your immediate, voluntary control, and the remaining 50% is habitual and genetic. That means that, no matter what your current life circumstances, you can dramatically shift your happiness immediately by asking the right questions. And you can shift it even more over time by choosing habits that promote happiness. Are you willing to become happier? This book can help.

Don't believe the myth "It just takes time." The truth is, releasing grief takes action.

30 MINUTES FOR GRIEF RELIEF

The process you will learn in this book, the Peace Method®, is a simple yet powerful coaching tool for going from pain to peace.

I have personally coached hundreds of people using the Peace Method®. My experience is that this process brings grief relief in 30 minutes or less. Typically, 15 minutes can bring insight and relief. Obviously, the person needs to want to feel better and be willing to release their grief.

I have never coached anyone who did not get some grief relief in 30 minutes. Sometimes the relief is slight, but many times it is profound, sometimes even life-changing. I will share real-life examples later in this book, with powerful results in 30 minutes or less.

Just as 30 minutes is ample time for you to take a shower and get clean, but that doesn't mean that you will only need to take one shower in your entire life, grief relief works the same way. If you are grieving, I recommend that you spend 30 minutes every day using the Peace Method®.

You can get good results by yourself, but it works much better when you have the support of a trained coach. At the Grief Coach Academy, we train coaches how to help their clients using the Peace Method® and many other coaching processes.

Grief is a normal and natural reaction to loss. If you are heartbroken, having a coach is not a "nice to have" but a necessary strategy to reclaim your happiness more quickly and easily. A certified coach trained at the Grief Coach Academy will lead you through a series of coaching processes designed to release grief, reclaim happiness, and create your ideal life.

Having a coach is like having a personal trainer at the gym. If you are committed, a good personal trainer will help you transform your body in a few months. It's the same with having a coach. If you are committed, a good coach will help you transform your happiness and your life in a few months.

The Peace Method® is like your favorite class at your gym. Like a fitness class that hits five major muscle groups, it is a well-rounded class. If you attend this one class faithfully, you will be fit in no time.

If you're ready to feel more peaceful, I invite you to use the Peace Method® every day for 30 minutes, and see what it does for you.

MY STORY

I don't think we can really hear another person until we know their story. So here is my story.

My life seemed like it couldn't get any better. My husband and I fell in love at university. We started with nothing. He was $14,000 in debt when we met, and I had maybe $500 to my name. But we were in love, and we wanted to be together, so we left our jobs and started a business together in our early twenties.

We needed a business that we could launch with no money, so we used his skill as a sailor and launched a yacht charter company. We managed the rental of sailboats owned by other people for a management fee.

I remember the first boat show we attended. The grizzled owners of other yacht charter companies dismissed our youthful enthusiasm and figured we wouldn't make it to the next boat show — we'd be out of business. Money ran out, my husband got a job to put groceries on the table, but we didn't give up on our dreams. From such humble beginnings, our company eventually grew to the largest yacht charter and yacht sales company in Western Canada — a multimillion dollar business. Our grizzled competitors were wrong.

A decade later, we were building our dream home on a lake at a world-class ski resort, Whistler, BC, Canada. I was following my dreams of being a writer and I had just met Mel Gibson, Goldie Hawn and John Badham (director of the movie *Stake Out*). As a result, I had just been hired to write my first script for real money. My husband and I had a four year-old son, who was adorable as only four-year-olds can be. In other words, life was great.

And then…my 33 year-old husband dropped dead.

It was completely unexpected. As you might imagine, my life completely shattered. I felt like Humpty Dumpty. My life as I knew it had shattered into a million pieces. And I couldn't put the pieces back together again.

My husband died beside me, so I had all these "if only's." If only the phone had been connected (he died the day we moved, and the phone wasn't connected yet). If only I'd known CPR. If only we had hired a mover. All these "if only's" kept me stuck in grief.

I didn't know how to work through all my feelings, so I kept writing in my diary. I have kept a diary since I was nine. I never intended to reread it myself, let alone show it to even one other person. I certainly never intended to publish it.

My diary was my own process of venting and expressing my feelings. It was my lifeline through grief. I needed some way to process and release my feelings.

About 10 years after my husband died, I stumbled across my old diary. I flipped it open, just intending to glance at it. But I couldn't put it down because it was so raw, so real. Two and a half hours later, I had read the whole thing. It revealed the overall process of grieving and healing.

I realized that I held in my hands the book that I had wanted to read when my heart was broken. I wanted a road map through the twists and turns of grief. I wanted to know when I would feel like myself again. I wanted to know, "Is this normal?" Grief is so intense. I had never experienced anything like it before.

It was a powerful and transformative journey. But there is a light at the end of the tunnel. Eventually, I went from heartbreak to happiness. You can, too.

I realized that my diary, which later became the book *From Heartbreak to Happiness* could be a lifeline for other heartbroken people. It could show them that there is hope for them, too. It could encourage them to hang in there, and let them know that they are not alone. That healing is a process.

My husband's death sent my life in a whole different direction. Through his death, he became my greatest spiritual teacher. Through his death, he profoundly changed me in ways that I'm deeply grateful for now. I now devote my life to helping other people go From Heartbreak to Happiness® more quickly and easily.

CHAPTER 1

THE PEACE METHOD®

ℰℴ

*External circumstances is not what draws us
into suffering. Suffering is caused and permitted
by an untamed mind.*
– The Dalai Lama

What the Peace Method® Can Do For You

The Peace Method® is a five-step process that can help you tame your mind. It can help you discover empowering possibilities. It can accelerate your healing. It has helped many people release grief, get unstuck, gain clarity, and decide on a productive course of action. Keep an open mind, try it out, and discover how it can help you, too.

THE PEACE METHOD® WILL HELP YOU

- Release grief
- Think clearly and calmly, even about challenging issues
- Dissolve any inner barriers to peace of mind
- Release limiting beliefs
- Embrace expansive, empowering beliefs
- Release the fear of intimacy and open your heart to love
- Make better decisions
- Reduce stress
- Take actions with clarity and enthusiasm
- Release the fear of failure or the fear of success
- Release self-sabotaging thoughts and behaviors
- Discover empowering possibilities
- Release financial fears and worry
- Shift to prosperity consciousness
- Feel good, happy and peaceful
- Empower you to proactively design and create your best possible life

The Peace Method® is easy to learn, easy to remember, and easy to use.

Overview

The Peace Method® is five simple steps from pain to peace. It is a great way to release grief. It will help you get unstuck in love, in loss, and in life.

I have used this process extensively as a coaching tool at the Grief Coach Academy, and have found it produces dramatic and sometimes even life-changing results in as little as fifteen minutes.

As Marianne Williamson, author of *A Return to Love* said, "A miracle is simply a shift in perception." The Peace Method®

methodically invites shifts of perception. It can alchemize pain into peace.

If you are using this process by yourself, write down your thoughts with each step. You can use the Peace Method® as a daily journaling process to gain peace of mind and clarity.

THE PEACE METHOD® STANDS FOR

P = Present Moment
E = Express Your Feelings
A = Accept and Appreciate
C = Consider the Contrary
E = Enthusiasm

"P" stands for present. So, the "P" in Peace Method® is a reminder to begin by coming into the present moment. Take a few deep breaths and get centered. (Even a few deep breaths can make a substantial difference. If you have more time, meditate for fifteen minutes.)

Notice if the perceived problem is in the present, past or future. We can never change the past. We can never solve all potential future problems. But we can deal with the one problem that is right here, right now. Problems are opportunities in disguise. The trick is to discover the opportunity.

The "E" stands for express your feelings. Invite your friend, family member, or coaching client to share their fears, worries, concerns and upset feelings. Or express your own feelings in your journal or to your coach. If you can't feel it, you can't heal it. So give yourself and others full permission to vent. What a gift it is to have a safe space to fully express your feelings and be understood before going on to any problem-solving activity!

The "A" stands for acceptance and appreciation. Stress is caused by resisting what is. When you resist what is, you feel like a victim. The past is not going to change, no matter how much you think it "should" be different. When you are resisting what is, you're not empowered. Acceptance is the opposite of denial.

Acceptance means that you make allowance for the reality of the current situation. By acceptance, I don't mean that you go completely limp and don't take action. Life is like martial arts. If someone comes at you with a blow, if you stay rigid and block it, the force of the blow is going to hit you hard. But if you see the blow coming and decide to work with the energy, you can deflect it or even turn it and use the energy to your advantage. Acceptance empowers you to discover the best possible response.

Appreciation takes this step even deeper. When you can discover something to appreciate, your sense of being victimized evaporates, and new possibilities emerge. The "A" step is complete if you can either accept or appreciate the situation.

The "C" stands for consider the contrary, or for rising to the challenge. If you're suffering, consider the contrary of your painful thought. Our minds work like a google search. If you type "black" into google, it is going to give you thousands of results for "black." When you type "white" into google, it will give you thousands of results for "white." Our minds work the same way. When we think painful thoughts, our minds will find plenty of evidence, and we get to be right—and disempowered. When we consider the contrary and investigate peaceful thoughts, our minds will also find evidence, and we also get to be right—and empowered. You can also use the "C" as an invitation to rise to challenge, and declare that you are going to meet and master this challenge.

The final "E" stands for enthusiasm. What can you choose to be enthusiastic about? This step invites you (or the person you're coaching) to make a conscious choice about some action to take, or a state of being to choose. This concludes the process with positive forward momentum and capitalizes on the wisdom and insight gained through the five steps of the Peace Method®.

Why Feeling Good is Important

Feeling good, or feeling calm and peaceful is not a "nice to have" but a "necessary strategy" in order to think clearly and make the best decisions.

People who are upset, fearful, grieving, anxious, heartbroken, or overwhelmed do not make good decisions. Actions taken when upset do not produce great results. The actions and results are inevitably tainted by the negativity.

On the other hand, when you are feeling calm and peaceful, you can see more possibilities, and think more clearly. You are then empowered to consciously choose the best possible response or action.

Even the most challenging situations — or I should say especially the most challenging situations — benefit from first taking a few moments to get calm. Actions taken from a place of calm clarity inevitably produce the best outcome.

Therefore, feeling good is not a luxury. It is an essential first step to achieving any goal.

You can use all five steps to gain clarity in just a few minutes, or you can explore each step in depth. We will be exploring each step in depth in this book, then I will give some examples from actual coaching sessions, so you can see the difference in clarity that these five steps have made to real people just like you.

CHAPTER 2

PEACE

❧

Nothing can bring you peace but yourself.
—Ralph Waldo Emerson

Peace is one of the most positive emotions that we can attain as normal human beings, which is why I called this process the Peace Method®. The name itself invites you to choose peace. The only higher state of being would be enlightenment, such as was attained by Jesus Christ or Buddha. While you have perhaps had moments of enlightenment, it is extraordinary. But we have all experienced moments of peace.

The ground-breaking book *Power vs Force* by David Hawkins, MD, PhD, changed the way I look at the world, and I urge you to read it. It contains a map of levels of consciousness and corresponding emotions, based upon an arbitrary scale from 1 to 1,000. The scale is logarithmic, so even a slight increase is significant. The emotions that feel bad are at the bottom, and the tipping point between feeling good and feeling bad is courage.

According to Dr. Hawkins' extensive research and testing using kinesiology, here is how different levels of consciousness or emotion stack up:

Ladder of Consciousness

600	Peace
540	Joy
500	Love
400	Reason
350	Acceptance, Forgiveness
300	Willingness
200	Courage
150	Anger
100	Fear
75	Grief
20	Shame

Source: *Power vs. Force* by Dr. Hawkins, MD, PhD

Notice that Grief is very near the bottom of the chart, at just 75 on this scale. The tipping point is Courage at 200. Everything below 200 is negative, everything above is positive.

In my experience, when people suffer a devastating loss such as a death or divorce, they suddenly fall down to grief (at 75). It's as though they were walking along in a park on a sunny day and then suddenly trip and fall down a well. It is dark in the well and the sides are slippery. They're stuck at the bottom of a well.

Many people get stuck in the well of grief for years—even decades. Most people don't know how to climb back up out of the well. It's not their fault. No one has taught them what to do.

A trained coach with the right coaching recipe can make an enormous difference. It's very helpful if someone shines a flashlight down the well, and says, "You're not alone. I'm here" and then throws them a rope ladder and talks them up the rungs of the rope ladder, step by step. Coaching processes like the Peace Method® are like rungs on the rope ladder back to freedom.

When people are grieving, the principle emotion is regret. Grief is not the lowest level. Guilt is lower. That's where you're blaming yourself, or blaming others. And shame is very close to death. That's where you're humiliated. The word "mortified" comes from the French word, "mort" which means death. So to be mortified is to have a little death.

When I'm coaching, I'm very conscious of Dr. Hawkin's scale. For example, it is not productive to shame ourselves or others. Shaming digs a deeper well. If we made a mistake, we should make amends and not do it again. It is counter-productive to shame ourselves or another person.

Dr. Hawkins says, "All truth is relative." When I first read that sentence, it blew my mind! How could that be so? I come from an academic family and had decades of education to teach me that truth is absolute, not relative. Yet, when I explored the perspective that "all truth is relative," it was useful and insightful. When I coach people through grief, their experience and point of view changes dramatically as they heal, and progress up the ladder from grief to acceptance, love and peace.

For example, let's talk about the death of a spouse. I'll use myself as an example. When my husband died suddenly at the age of 33, I was grieving. Then I actually slipped down to guilt and shame. Let's start at the bottom and see what each level sounds like as we work our way up Dr. Hawkin's ladder of consciousness.

EXAMPLE: DEATH OF A SPOUSE

---

20 (Shame) — I can't even grieve right, I can't get my act together.

30 (Guilt) — It's my fault. If only I'd known CPR, he'd be alive.

50 (Hopeless) — My situation is hopeless. Despair.

75 (Grief) — Life is tragic, friendless, forlorn. Regret.

100 (Fear) — How are we going to survive?

125 (Desire) — Frustration, "Why doesn't someone help us?"

150 (Anger) — I'm furious that my son is without his father. I'm angry I have to struggle as a single Mom — that was not the plan.

175 (Pride) — I deserve better. My son deserves better. I am going to create a good future. I refuse to be a victim of these circumstances.

200 (Courage) — I am capable and competent. I can handle this.

250 (Neutrality) — If not the future I planned, then the future God planned.

310 (Willingness) — I'm willing to learn and grow.

350 (Acceptance) — I accept his death. I'm grateful for the time we shared.

400 (Reason) — People die. It happens at all ages.

500+ (Love) — The world looks interesting, friendly, and lovable. I have the gift of new eyes, a fresh perspective. I'm overflowing with love.

600 (Peace) — Spirits are immortal. Death is an illusion.

For example, when I was vibrating with shame (20), I blamed myself. I thought I wasn't even grieving right, that my life was in shambles and I wasn't getting my act together. I felt shame.

When I felt guilt (30), I blamed myself for my husband's death. If only I'd known better CPR, if only we'd hired a mover, if only the phones had been connected, he would be alive. Guilt was like flypaper keeping me stuck.

Sometimes I felt things were hopeless (50), and I despaired. My son would never have his father alive again; I would never be with my soul mate again.

When I was grieving (75), I felt that life was tragic. I felt alone and forlorn. I felt regret over the holidays we didn't take, and grieved over present and future losses. My husband would not attend our son's graduation or wedding, would never see his grandchildren.

When I was afraid (100), I was anxious about how I would be able to pay the bills and support our little family of two. I felt afraid that I would be unable to both be a good mom and a good provider.

At 125 or desire I felt frustrated. Why doesn't somebody help us? I felt frustrated that I couldn't write all day and night to become a great writer and establish a successful career and also be a good Mom.

At 150, which is anger, I was furious that my husband had abandoned me, furious that I had to deal with being a single Mom, furious that our son didn't have his father. I was furious with myself for failing to prevent my husband's death.

At 175, which is pride, I knew I deserved better. I was determined to create a good future. I refused to be a victim of these circumstances. My will hardened into resolve. I was going to do whatever it took to overcome this challenge.

At courage (200), which is the tipping point towards positive emotions, I would literally repeat the mantra, "I am capable and competent. I can handle this."

At neutrality (250), I surrendered my attachment to my vision for my future. If not the future I planned, then the future God planned. Thy will be done.

At willingness (310), I was willing to learn and grow. I was eager to learn and receptive to coaching. I was willing to work hard to make our house a home, to make our family strong.

At acceptance (350), I accepted his death as if I had chosen it. This happened in a dream on the second anniversary of his death. This dream changed my life, and you can read about it in my book *From Heartbreak to Happiness*®. With acceptance, I was grateful for the time we shared. I was grateful for our son. I was grateful that I didn't know that he would die young, so that the time we did have together was not tainted with dread.

At reason (400), I understood that people die. And sometimes people die young. It was no longer a punishment. It's just logically what happens.

When I was vibrating with love (500+), I was grateful to be alive. The world looked friendly, then lovable. I felt that I was living in a supportive Universe.

At the level of peace (600), I knew that souls are immortal. Death is an illusion.

I find these levels of consciousness from Dr. Hawkin's excellent book *Power vs. Force* a useful and profound way to understand the phases of healing from grief. My book *From Heartbreak to Happiness* is just one person's diary of healing, but it reveals that healing grief is not a linear process. Even shortly after David's death, I sometimes experienced higher levels of consciousness such as love and peace.

How do you respond differently when you feel grief, anger, acceptance, willingness, love, or peace? What is your experience? What brings the best results?

I come from an academic family. Those of us who have been blessed (or cursed) with academic training need to understand that reason (the 400s in Dr. Hawkin's work) is only one layer of truth. It can be helpful, but only to explain things to the mind. Heartbreak is not about a broken head, it is about a broken heart. You can't talk somebody out of grief using logic.

The key to solving any challenge is to first get peaceful.

Things that Rob Us of Peace

Many situations upset our peace: death, divorce, breakups, job loss, bankruptcy, having a special needs child with autism, having an aging parent with Alzheimer's, a diagnosis of cancer.

But it is not our life circumstances that destroy our ability to see clearly and take the right action. It is our thinking. Stressful thoughts trigger stressful emotions.

When we are engulfed with grief, regret, fear, or panic, we cannot think clearly. We flood our body with adrenalin—which is great for fleeing from a saber-tooth tiger, but counter-productive for solving most of the challenges of modern life.

While we may not be able to change our life circumstances, we can empower ourselves to make wise choices by defusing our reactive emotions. Then we can peacefully consider the situation.

Let's examine each of the five steps of Peace Method®.

CHAPTER 3

PRESENT

ℰℴ

*If you embrace the present and become one with it, and merge with it,
you will experience a fire, a glow, a sparkle of ecstasy throbbing in
every living sentient being. As you begin to experience this exultation
of spirit in everything that is alive, as you become intimate with it,
joy will be born within you, and you will drop the terrible burdens
and encumbrances of defensiveness, resentment, and hurtfulness.
Only then will you become lighthearted, carefree, joyous, and free.*
—Deepak Chopra

The "P" in the Peace Method® reminds you to be fully
present. The present is your point of power. As the Buddha said,
"Do not dwell in the past, do not dream of the future, concentrate
the mind on the present moment."

You can never change the past. You can never solve all
potential future problems. But you can deal with the one challenge
or opportunity that is right here, right now. And you do that best
when you are calm and centered.

The "P" in the Peace Method® invites you to breathe deeply
and consciously. Come fully into the present moment. Then
determine what the present actually contains, so that you can be
proactive—not reactive.

Be like a mirror. A mirror beautifully reflects the present
moment. It is not stained or tarnished with the images it reflected
yesterday. It does not think it is the images that it reflects.

So often when people are upset, they are not in the present. They are regretting the past, or anticipating the future with anxiety.

Trying to solve all potential future problems is an insane recipe for never-ending stress. It's like interest on money you haven't even borrowed yet. Or as Martha Beck put it, "It's only when I try to anticipate the future that I feel like I'm losing my mind."

As someone once told me, "The past is history, the future is a mystery, and this moment is a gift. That is why it is called the present."

When you are fully present, you give others the gift of your presence. As Eckhart Tolle, author of *The Power of Now* said, "Being present is infinitely more powerful than anything one could say or do, although sometimes being present can give rise to words or actions."

In his wonderful book *Peace is Every Step* Thich Nhat Hanh wrote, "The most precious gift we can offer others is our presence. When mindfulness embraces those we love, they will bloom like flowers."

Here are a few questions to consider:

- Are you fully present? Calm, peaceful and centered? (If not, take a few deep, calming breaths right now.)
- Is this painful thought about the present? Or it is a fearful anticipation of some possible future outcome? Or is it about the past?
- Is this upset emotion about the present? Or is it regret about something that happened in the past? Or fear about something that might happen in the future?
- What's the reality of the present situation?
- It is true? Are you sure? Where is your proof?
- Can you change this?
- What are the possibilities here? What choices do you have?
- Is now a good time to think about it constructively and productively? Or are you worrying, fretting or stewing at 3

am? Worrying is not thinking. Turn your worries over to God. Schedule time for thinking.

- How can it get better than this?
- How does the present situation match or contrast with your goal?
- What actions can be taken in the present moment?
- What resources can you use to deal with this challenge?
- What can you learn?
- Who knows what you need to know?
- Who can provide coaching or emotional support?
- What questions can you ask to create something better?

The next time you are upset, notice. Are you fully present?

You Can Never Solve All Potential Future Problems

For decades, I thought the reasonable and rational thing to do was to anticipate all future problems and solve them proactively. I was wearing myself out.

Then I read *The Power of Now* by Eckhart Tolle. He wrote, "You can never solve all potential future problems." That sentence leapt out at me. It changed my life. I desperately needed some new wisdom, and a kinder and gentler approach than beating myself up for all my "mistakes."

A few years after my husband's death, in spite of my attempts to anticipate potential future problems and "head them off at the pass" I was facing a problem that could lead to bankruptcy.

After investing considerable time and effort and lot more money than I'd initially intended, I completed a beautiful renovation of the house that my late husband built. I invested more money than was wise because I was working through my grief about the "dream house" that David built, yet never saw completed. It felt like a shattered dream, and in some ways looked like a shattered dream. Renovating the house renovated my heart. Emotionally, the renovation was healing and cathartic.

However, the process emptied my bank accounts. I then sold the house on a lease-option, and it seemed that I could close that chapter of my life. Big sigh of relief!

I thought the substantial down payment of $150,000 would keep the buyers honest and committed. A lengthy contract anticipated potential future problems and addressed them proactively. For example, the contract stipulated that they would not sublet, and that I would maintain the security service that detected entry, freezing temperatures, fire, and intruders.

In spite of my precautions, it appeared that the purchasers of my home decided to breach the contract and sublet the ski chalet over Christmas. Perhaps to cover this fact up, it seemed that someone disabled the security system.

The power failed, the pipes in the house froze, then burst. In the ensuing flood, the entire ground floor of the house was destroyed, to the tune of six figures of damage. This put the lease-option purchasers in breach of contract, jeopardized the sale as well as the insurance coverage, and the whole thing was an enormous mess—literally, financially, legally, and emotionally.

My nerves were frayed, and I was stewing about "mistakes" I had made in the past, and anxious about all the things that could go wrong in the future.

Fortunately, at the time I was reading *The Power of Now*. Eckhart Tolle's words "You can never solve all potential future problems" freed me from the crushing burden of trying to solve all potential future problems. For every problem I solved, my mind could think of a dozen more problems that could occur, writhing like venomous snakes in Medusa's hair. Trying to solve all potential future problems is insane.

The path to peaceful sanity is to deal with the present moment proactively, and accept that the future is unknown and unknowable.

In case you're curious, in the end, the buyers walked. I renovated the house yet again. As I put the house back together, my frayed relationship with my then-fiancé came apart. By the time I finally sold the house almost two years later, it sold for a million dollars less than it had formerly been appraised for. At the time, it was stressful. The more I stayed in the present, the more I was able to take care of the things that needed to be done with peaceful productivity.

We can never solve all potential future problems. Never! So give it up, it's a lost cause. If you wait until you have solved all potential future problems, you'll never be happy.

My suggestion is, deal with the two or three most probable things. Take action to offset that risk. For example, get car insurance and life insurance, and write your will. Don't postpone being happy until everything is done, because it is never all done.

The present moment is the path to happiness. The present moment is the only point at which you can choose things that will create the future that you want.

Some ways to access the present moment follow.

Breathing as a Doorway to the Present

Here's an example of a brief meditation that I created. In just four breaths, you can bring yourself into a more peaceful place.

Breathe in Divine Love…Be Divine Love…
Exhale, radiating Divine Love
Breathe in Divine Light….Be Divine Light….
Exhale, radiating Divine Light
Breathe in Divine Power….Be Divine Power….
Exhale, radiating Divine Power
Breathe in Divine Peace….Be Divine Peace….
Exhale, radiating Divine Peace

Here's another brief meditation by Thich Nhat Hanh, a Buddhist monk.

Breathing in, I calm my body.
Breathing out, I smile.
Dwelling in the present moment,
I know it is a wonderful moment!

In just a few breaths, you can use a brief meditation to center yourself or your coaching client in the present moment.

I recommend a minimum of 15 minutes of deep breathing as a daily practice. Ideally, meditate twice a day at sunrise and sunset. Close your eyes and focus your attention on the space in your head between your eyes. Or focus your attention on a single candle flame. Choosing a daily habit of deep breathing or meditation will gradually deepen your sense of peace.

Meditation as a Doorway to the Present

Meditation has shown promising results in altering brain wave patterns as well as growing new brain cells that are the product of inner mindfulness. Studies published in the NeuroReport journal in November 2005 showed that meditation increased grey matter in participants, all of whom were average, normal people with jobs and families who meditated only 40 minutes a day.

I recently interviewed Dr. Joe Dispenza, and I highly recommend his book *Evolve Your Brain* for a deeper look at the science behind your brain health. The bottom line is, you don't have to be a Buddhist monk to benefit from mediation. It not only grows more brain cells, but may also slow the age-related thinning of the frontal cortex. Mediation will expand your peace of mind.

Here is an example of a mediation I used at a recent Grief Coach Academy coach training event to bring all the attendees into the present moment.

CENTERING MEDITATION

Take a couple of deep, cleansing breaths and release. Put your conscious awareness on your body, and feel the life within your body. Take another deep breath ... and release.

I invite you to come fully into the present moment. Come into the here and now. This is your point of power; this is the point from which you can create the life you desire.

So take a deep breath. Relax your body, exhale and smile. Inhale, coming fully into the present moment. Exhale, knowing it's a wonderful moment.

And again, inhale and relax your body. Exhale and smile. Inhale, coming fully into the present moment. And exhale, knowing it's a wonderful moment. And again, breathing at your own pace, relaxing your body. Smile.

Coming fully into the present moment, knowing it's a wonderful moment.

I invite you to continue deep breathing while I state my intention for our time together today.

I honor and acknowledge that the Divine is. It is love and light. It is that peace that surpasses all understanding. It is wisdom, creativity, joy, connection. I honor and acknowledge that the Divine is in you and in me. I invite that part of us that is Divine, or that part of us that is an instrument or channel for the Divine to be fully present right here and right now.

May you be blessed on your journey from heartbreak to happiness. May you relax into a deeper knowing of your Divine purpose. Relax into the peace of mind, the joy and happiness that is your Divine birthright. Relax into knowing that you are not your feelings, you are not your thoughts, you are not your story, you are not all the events that have happened to you. You are a Divine spiritual being having a human experience.

Relax into, surrender into receiving all the gifts of wisdom that are here for you, even if those gifts of wisdom sometimes show up like your feelings being triggered, your grief being triggered.

Relax into knowing that life is a gift. I invite you to be willing to get what you came for. I invite you to be willing to remember that you are a Divine being here on an amazing Divine mission. I invite you to be willing to remember who you truly are. Know that it's your birthright to be happy, peaceful, and prosperous. It's your birthright to contribute to the world in amazing ways while you feel connected and have deep, meaningful relationships. All is well in your world.

I release this intention with gratitude and with thanksgiving, knowing that it was already done even before I asked. So be it, and so it is.

When I am coaching my clients, I begin each call with a brief meditation to bring my client into the present moment. Although it only takes a few minutes, I often notice that my client's energy shifts dramatically from anxiety to peace.

As a coach trainer, I recommend that coaches begin each coaching session by bringing their client into the present moment. When you're coaching, it's wonderful to be reminded that you don't need the answers. It brings peace of mind to invite in Divine support and remind yourself that your client is Divine, too, and has their own wisdom, their own answers.

I begin each day with meditation, and find that it centers me. One mediation I love is the Buddhist loving-kindness meditation, which I learned from Jack Kornfield. I invite you to try it as a daily ritual. Focus first on filling yourself with loving-kindness for five minutes or so. Then turn your attention to sending loving-kindness to your family, friends, and clients. Then you can extend your attention to neutral people, and difficult people.

LOVING-KINDNESS MEDITATION

May I be filled with loving-kindness.
May I be safe from inner and outer dangers.
May I be well in body and mind.
May I be at ease and happy.

May you be filled with loving-kindness.
May you be safe from inner and outer dangers.
May you be well in body and mind.
May you be at ease and happy.

MEDITATION FOR COMPASSION

May you be held in compassion.
May your pain and sorrow be eased.
May you be at peace.

You are not trying to fix anyone, but merely to hold sorrow and pain with tender compassion. After you have sent this compassion to others, send it to yourself.

MEDITATION FOR PEACE

Breathing in, I calm my body.
Breathing out, I calm my mind.
May I be balanced.
May I be at peace.
May I learn to see the arising and passing
of all things with equanimity and balance.
May I be open and balanced and peaceful.

Repeat the first four lines until you feel calm and peaceful. Then you can consider that all things pass away—buildings, plants, animals, people. Expand the meditation to include the last two lines as you gently consider the impermanent and precious nature of life.

These Buddhist meditations can help you deepen your peace. Select the one you like the best, and use it as a daily meditation practice for the next 30 days.

Walking as a Doorway into the Present

At Grief Coach Academy coach training events, I often invite the participants to go on a morning walk and drink in the beauty of the natural surroundings.

I invite you to go for a walking meditation. Simply follow these instructions:

WALKING MEDITATION INSTRUCTIONS

Imagine that you are a visitor from another planet. This is your very first day on planet Earth. Your very first day in your body. Notice how it feels to walk, to breathe, how the air feels on your skin.

As you walk, notice everything. Notice how everything seems alive, even the very earth you walk upon. Name everything. You are a collector. Everything you appreciate, acknowledge, savor, you get to keep forever. Everything you take for granted is lost to you forever. Walk in silence.

One busy female executive I'll call Amanda shared her awe after doing the walking meditation two mornings in a row.

Amada shared, "I discovered I had taken a lot for granted on the first day. I was astounded at the sights, smells, textures, feelings that I had completely missed the first day. I walked about eight feet and would see four things that I had just missed completely the first day! I wandered around in awe and curiosity about what's in my life, what's right in front of my face that I'm taking for granted."

This walking meditation is a beautiful metaphor for our lives; we rush through our lives to get it "done." When you're done, you're dead. That's the end. So we're rushing and we're missing all the gifts in front of us. This moment is all you have. And if you really receive it, what a gift!

Fresh Eyes as a Doorway to the Present

Looking at things with fresh eyes can transform your experience.

I'd like to share a passage from my book *From Heartbreak to Happiness* which is my intimate diary of healing after my husband died suddenly at the age of thirty-three. I wrote this diary entry 204 days after my husband died.

THE GIFT OF NEW EYES

It is such an exquisitely beautiful day. As I drive, my eyes feast on the flowers flanking the avenue: roses, salvia, hydrangea. Each flower seems more delightful than the last.

I mentally breathe in the vibrant colors and beauty. I gradually become intoxicated – head over heels in love with Life and all its expressions of beauty.

A hillside stretches before me, like a puppy on its back, squirming to have its tummy rubbed. I can't resist the invitation.

I park, then gallop like a frisky colt on the lawn, exulting in this precious moment. I'm intoxicated with love, with delight, with the extraordinary gift of this day – no, not this day – just this single amazing moment.

I breathe it in. I breathe it all in, greedy to imprint the intense yellow of the dandelion, the delicate pink of the tiny daisy, the rainbow dancing in the dewdrop, the succulent green of the grass. I soak in the sunshine kissing my skin, the warm caress of the breeze. I'm greedy to see it,

*smell it, feel it, hear it, taste it, appreciate and love it all —
and never forget.*

*For who knows if this will be my last day on
Earth? Who knows if I shall ever see a hillside quite so
lovely ever again? Who knows if the memory of this
moment will have to nourish me forever?*

Mindfulness as a Doorway into the Present

*My friends, it is through the establishment of the lovely
clarity of mindfulness that you can let go of grasping after
the past and future, overcome attachment and grief,
abandon all clinging and anxiety, and awaken an
unshakable freedom of heart, here, now.*
— Buddha

It requires mindfulness to stay in the present moment. For
example, I recently attended the wedding of my best friend's son.
The ceremony was lovely, and the day was filled with friendly faces.
When I was fully present, I had a great time. When I left the present
moment, musing about my own wedding, and how my own hopes
for a happy future together were dashed with my husband's sudden
death, I missed the joy of the present moment. The past was casting
a shadow over it.

Or when I felt envy and noticed thoughts such as "It's too
late for me — I'll never get married again and experience this joy of
starting a life together" I robbed myself of the joy available in the
present moment. Projections about the future were obscuring the
delight available in the moment.

Can you relate? The good news is, these thoughts are not our
enemies but our friends. Notice when your thoughts are pulling you
out of the present moment. Give thanks for your conscious
awareness. Then take a breath, and bring your awareness back to
your body, back to the present. Savor the moment that is in front of
you.

The only path to joy, happiness, love and prosperity is through the present moment. Any practice of mindfulness can bring you fully into the present. Doing one thing at a time will deepen your peace. When you are making dinner, be fully present as you chop the vegetables—rather than anticipating the meal. When you are eating, don't anticipate the dishes. When you are doing the dishes, be fully present and enjoy the soap and hot water.

When you are eating, savor your food. Smell it, taste it. Chew slowly, be mindful of the flavors, textures, aromas. We are programmed to get things done, even eating. Scientists have studied the pleasure that we get from eating. Over 90% of the pleasure is in the first bite. So I really invite you to fully savor the first bite, and every bite. If you bring full awareness into your meals, you will enjoy your food much more—and you will be satiated with the right amount of food for your body. Over-eating comes when we do not pay attention.

Mindfulness is patient, receptive, non-judging awareness. "Mindfulness does not reject experience. It lets experience be the teacher," writes Jack Kornfield, Buddhist teacher, psychologist, and author of the wonderful book *The Wise Heart*. I highly recommend this book as well as *Peace is Every Step* by Thich Nhat Hanh if you'd like to explore mindfulness more deeply.

Your Body as a Doorway into the Present

Move your body the way you'd like to feel. Get moving! Exercise every day. Walk tall, sit up straight, smile!

Nobel Prize winner Daniel Kahneman reports in his book *Thinking Fast and Slow* that being amused tends to make you smile — but also smiling tends to make you feel amused. An experiment asked college students to hold a pencil in their mouth. Those who held it sideways in their mouth like a horse's bit were forced to smile. Those who held it pointing forward in pursed lips were forced to frown. When they were asked to rate the humor from cartoons, those who were "smiling" (without any awareness of doing so) found the cartoons funnier than those who were "frowning." Daniel Kahneman concludes, "You can see why the common admonition to "act calm and kind regardless of how you feel" is very good advice: you are likely to be rewarded by actually feeling calm and kind."

You can also become aware of the energy in your body as you breathe deeply. Notice the energy in your feet, your legs, your abdomen, all the way up your body. Send loving energy and gratitude to your body.

After all, if you were in agony with a toothache, you would be extremely grateful for the toothache to stop. If you were suddenly blind, you would mourn the loss of your precious sight. If you were unable to walk, you would marvel at the simple miracle of being able to walk. If your heart stopped beating, all your pressing appointments would be cancelled. So be grateful now.

I invite you to notice that your body breathes by itself, the heart beats by itself, the food digests by itself, your hair grows by itself, your blood circulates by itself. Your body takes you everywhere you want to go, 99% of the time, without a single complaint.

And yet often we only notice that one percent of the time when it says "Feed me. Sleep me. Touch me." And the other 99 percent, we usually take for granted the miraculous gifts we've been given.

Especially women, when we look in the mirror we only see things to criticize: oh, that wrinkle, oh, that grey hair, oh that belly. And we forget how wonderful it is to have a body.

We've all been given these amazing "rental cars" for the period of our stay on planet Earth. Your body is your Lamborghini, your Ferrari, your Mercedes. Wow! How many of us appreciate our car more than our body? I invite you to remember what a sacred gift your body is, and send it loving gratitude. Take care of it, appreciate it.

Prayer as a Doorway into the Present

A powerful prayer or affirmation can also bring us into the present. Here are a couple of my favorites.

PRAYER BY ST. FRANCIS OF ASSISI

Lord, make me an instrument of Your peace.
Where there is hatred, let me sow love;
Where there is injury, pardon;
Where there is doubt, faith;
Where there is darkness, light;
And where there is sadness, joy;
O Divine Master, grant that I may not so much seek
To be consoled as to console;
To be understood as to understand;
To be loved as to love;
For it is in giving that we receive;
It is in pardoning that we are pardoned;
And it is in dying to self that we are born to eternal light.

Here are some powerful words the from the Buddhist tradition, this time from the 16th century sage Shantideva. Bodhisattva is the Sanskrit word for a being who is devoted to awakening and acting for the benefit of all that lives. The way of the Bodhisattva is one of the most powerful of all the Buddhist forms of practice. It is radical in that it states that our highest happiness comes only from serving the welfare of others as well as ourself. These are the Bodhisattva vows taken by the Dalai Lama.

BODHISATTVA VOWS BY SHANTIDEVA

May I be a guard for those who need protection
A guide for those on the path
A boat, a raft, a bridge for those who wish to cross the flood
May I be a lamp in the darkness

A resting place for the weary
A healing medicine for all who are sick
A vase of plenty, a tree of miracles
And for the boundless multitudes of living beings
May I bring sustenance and awakening
Enduring like the earth and the sky
Until all beings are freed from sorrow
And all are awakened.

CHAPTER 4

EXPRESS YOURSELF

❧

Express yourself completely, then keep quiet.
Be like the forces of nature: when it blows, there is only wind;
when it rains, there is only rain;
when the clouds pass, the sun shines through. ...
If you open yourself to insight,
you are at one with insight and you can use it completely.
If you open yourself to loss, you are at one with loss,
and you can accept it completely.
— Lao-tzu, Tao de Ching (tr. Stephen Mitchell)

Expressing your feelings is the next step in the Peace Method®. This is ancient wisdom, as Lao-tzu wrote in the *Tao de Ching* around the 6th century BC. Like the beauty in nature, there is beauty in authentic self-expression.

Unexpressed Feelings are Toxic

Putting off dealing with your feelings is like putting off doing your taxes. They don't go away and the consequences and penalties just get worse and worse.

It is essential to our well-being that we express our true feelings. Paradoxically, by expressing our feelings, we get to release them. When we "stuff" or deny our feelings, we get to keep them.

Unexpressed feelings are like food poisoning. Imagine two people go out for sushi dinner, and they both get food poisoning. The one that throws up gets what was bothering her out of her system. She soon feels better. The one that decides to "stuff it" keeps the poison inside. He suffers, and may even die from the toxins.

As with food poisoning, we feel bad when we "stuff it." We often resist sharing feelings such as grief, despair, shame or anger. Many people "stuff" their feelings. We know it's going to be a little messy. And yet when we keep such feelings inside, we keep the toxins inside, we keep the poison inside. And the poison affects us in many ways. It can damage our health, wealth, happiness, and relationships.

If we let the toxic feelings out, it can be messy in the moment. Just as when we have food poisoning and we throw up, it's messy. But it is also life-saving. You need to get whatever is bothering you out of your system.

Stuffing our feelings has shocking consequences. One study reported that women who stuffed their feelings during marital arguments were four times more likely to <u>die</u> during a 10-year period. That study followed over 4,000 married adults over ten years and was reported in *Bottom Line Health* May 2008. Surprisingly, stuffing your feelings can literally kill you.

Listening is the oldest form of healing. Listening is a huge gift. You don't need to give your friend, family member, or coaching client the answer. When you listen, you allow them to express their feelings. When you listen to others, you are increasing their health, wellbeing and longevity. That's a huge gift. That's a bigger gift than handing them the solution to their problem.

Fixing another person's problems is not a gift, it is disempowering. Let them find their own solution and discover their own wisdom.

If you find that your friends and family cannot hold the space for you to fully and authentically express your thoughts and feelings, I highly recommend getting a coach. Not only will a great coach listen, they will walk you through a step-by-step process designed to help you. In my experience, when you are facing major change, having a coach is not merely a "nice to have" but a necessary strategy.

You are Not Your Thoughts or Feelings

It's essential to your well-being that you express your true feelings. Sometimes the farther you come along the path towards self-actualization, the more danger there is that you can get your pride involved, and not be willing to admit your authentic feelings. Perhaps you've achieved a life-long goal and have become a published author, a coach who makes a significant difference in the lives of others, or a CEO running a successful business. Perhaps you feel pretty good about how much you've grown, how peaceful you've become.

We're all human beings. We are all very much the same. No matter how successful, no matter how spiritual, we all face challenges and heartbreak from time to time.

Freedom comes from being willing to be authentic. If you need other people's approval, you will be their prisoner. You are not your thoughts, you are not your feelings. Invite thoughts and feelings to pass through you. Don't get too attached.

I'd like to uncouple your value from your emotions. Take your right hand and make a fist. Now hold that fist out in front of you at shoulder height. Hold it steady. It's solid like a rock. That's who you are. Your worth as a child of God is unwavering.

Now take your left hand and hold it at shoulder height as well. This hand represents your feelings. Now your feelings are aligned with your rock-solid God-given value as a human being. Now imagine you've been fired from your job. Your right hand is solid, but your left hand dips. You feel sad, you feel worried.

Now, imagine that you find a great job that pays you twice as much. Now you feel happy—and your left hand will rise to reflect that. Now you get divorced, and your left hand dips. Now you fall in love, and your left hand rises again. Life is like this, your emotions go up and down like the tides, but your true value as a human being is constant.

You are not your feelings. You are not your thoughts.

Your Thoughts are Like a Software Program Running Your Life

So many people hesitate to admit that they have limiting beliefs about happiness, relationships, success, money, and many other things. Unfortunately, what you don't express can—and does—hurt you. Your unexpressed limiting beliefs run your life, your bank account, and your relationships like a powerful software program running invisibly in the background.

For example, you will not make more money than your beliefs allow. Or, if you do, you will quickly self-sabotage, and not keep it.

This is why lottery winners who win millions of dollars end up broke a few years later. Their belief is that they don't deserve to be millionaires, and so they create that reality and return to their "comfort zone" of poverty even after receiving a huge, unexpected windfall of millions of dollars.

Our beliefs are extremely powerful. They are running invisibly in the background like the software programs used by your computer. The good news is that you can rewrite the code using the Peace Method®.

But first you need to become aware of all the limiting "code" that was "pre-installed" by people such as your parents, your school, your church, your community, and others. Once you become aware of limiting beliefs, you can investigate them, challenge them, and rewrite them to more liberating, expansive, and prosperous beliefs.

In my experience, words are either blessings or curses. Words are extremely powerful. Use deliberate, conscious word choice to create your desired future.

As Mark Twain said, "A powerful agent is the right word. Whenever we come upon one of those intensely right words…the resulting effect is physical as well as spiritual, and electrically prompt."

We curse ourselves when we repeat painful thoughts or limiting beliefs. Scientists have discovered that the average person has about 66,000 thoughts per day, and nearly 80% of these thoughts are negative.

These often-repeated negative thoughts are sabotaging your happiness and success. It is imperative that you interrupt this toxic self-talk deliberately and methodically.

Three Thoughts Deepen Despair

Three kinds of thoughts deepen despair. Thinking that the problem is personal, permanent or pervasive is a recipe for heartbreak. These are "red flag" thoughts.

PERSONAL

When you think that a problem is personal, you think "it's my fault" or "this is all about me." Thinking the problem is personal is going to deepen your despair as you add guilt and blame and shame to an already-heartbreaking situation. Listen for shaming and blaming words. "Should" is one of the most violent words in the English language.

For example, there's a huge difference between getting fired at work and thinking, "Oh my God, this is all my fault" and spinning into regret and rumination, versus thinking, "The company probably needs to lay off people because times are tough, profit is down, overhead is too high." That is a more balanced perspective that is more likely to bring peace of mind and empower constructive action. It de-personalizes it.

Or you might have a special needs child and think, "Oh my God, what did I do to deserve this? I must have done something wrong when I was pregnant." Rather than seeing the situation as entirely personal, a more peaceful perspective would be to notice that a certain percentage of children are born with special needs. "Why me?" can then become, "Why not me?"

Martha Beck is an amazing author who wrote a memoir called *Expecting Adam*, which is a very powerful story about her pregnancy. She knew that she was carrying a baby with Down's syndrome. Against the wishes of many of her friends and family, she decided to carry the baby to term. She was firm in her stance: This is my child, I'm not going to abort. She could have blamed herself and created anguish and suffering. But instead she allowed this amazing baby to come into her life. Adam was a gift, not a curse. He blessed her and changed her profoundly in wonderful ways.

Using my own story as an example, at first I thought God must hate me to take my husband away at the age of 33. I thought my husband's death was personal. That it was my fault. Later, I understood with greater wisdom that my late husband's death was his life path, not mine. I understood that although I was impacted by his death, I am not the center of the Universe. David had his own life, and his own death. Realizing that his death was not sent as a personal punishment allowed my soul to grow.

When you notice that you are thinking that a problem is 100% your fault, seek a more balanced and empowering perspective so that you don't get stuck in despair and guilt. Mistakes call for correction, never punishment.

PERMANENT

No matter how extreme a situation is, it will change. It cannot continue forever. Thus, a great forest fire is always destined to burn itself out; a turbulent sea will become calmer. Natural events balance themselves out by seeking their opposites, and this process of balance is at the heart of all healing.... That is why, even in the midst of an extreme situation, the wise are patient. Whether the situation is

*illness, calamity, or their own anger, they know that
healing will follow upheaval.*
— Deng Ming-Dao, author *365 Tao*

Don't think your life situation is permanent. Everything is subject to change. Remember, "This too shall pass."

For example, if you think, "I'm single and I'll always be single" that's thinking that being single is permanent. Listen for words like "always" and "never." Those are "red flag" words.

When you think "Well, I'm single today, who knows what tomorrow holds?" That's much lighter.

What if the truth always makes you feel lighter and a lie will always makes you feel heavier?

If you think, "My house is in foreclosure and I'll always be broke," you're thinking that the situation is permanent. That's not helpful. Instead, ask yourself, "How could I create financial freedom?" If you decide that you are going to create a solid financial future for yourself, that kind of thinking will produce desirable results. Thinking that the situation is permanent (and therefore hopeless) will not.

PERVASIVE

When you think the situation is pervasive, you believe that it will contaminate every part of your life, every quadrant.

Pervasive might sound like, "My husband died, I'm a bad person, God hates me, and it's going to affect everything. I'm not ever going to be able to make a living again, I'm not going to be a good mom, we'll always have a broken family." With thoughts like that, it's not surprising if the person doesn't want to get out of bed!

Pervasive stacks up one heartbreak onto another onto another. It is far wiser to deal with one thing at a time. That's more manageable. Separate each challenge, give it your attention, investigate it, and come up with an action plan to address it.

If you are thinking the situation is personal, permanent, and pervasive that's a recipe for despair. Life looks bleak and hopeless. You might even feel suicidal.

When you hear yourself or others making statements containing any of these three dangerous kinds of thinking, those are red flags. Stop yourself, stop others. Challenge that painful thought. A simple way to challenge is to ask, "Is that true?" You may notice that it is not a fact, just a theory. That can create an immediate shift in perception.

Defensiveness

Completely desist from the defending your point of view. When you have no point to defend you do not allow the birth of an argument. If you do this consistently, if you stop fighting and resisting, you will fully experience the present, which is a gift.
— Deepak Chopra, author *The Seven Spiritual Laws of Success*

Notice when you're feeling defensive, feeling attacked, feeling that you want to justify your behavior. That is normal. Your ego has been triggered. There is no need to make it wrong. Simply notice, and breathe into it. Come back into the present moment and choose to let those upset feelings pass on by.

A lot of our energy goes into upholding our sense of importance. If you were willing to let go of even a little of that need, you would have access to abundant energy to create the life of your dreams.

It's not your business what other people think of you. That's freeing, so you can just be you. And that's the best choice anyway. There is only one you. So express your beautiful, unique, amazing self.

As Dr. Dain Heer recommends in his book *Being You, Changing the World* asking yourself "Who does this belong to?" for three days can change your life. You may discover that most of the painful thoughts, feelings, and beliefs you experience are not even yours! They were passed on to you by your parents, teachers, or others. You are free to let them go.

Thoughts vs. Feelings

It's important to discern the difference between thoughts and feelings, so that you can get in touch with your authentic feelings, and help your coaching client do the same. Upset feelings reveal unmet needs.

For example, if a frustrated wife says, "I feel I am living with a wall" that is not a feeling, but a thought. If she expressed her feelings, it could sound like, "I feel lonely" (when you don't talk to me). Her thought is, "My husband shuts me out." Her need is for greater connection.

If an upset business partner says, "I feel that you are taking advantage of me" that is not a feeling, but a thought. The thought is, "You are taking advantage of me." The feeling is "I feel angry and upset" (when you don't work as many hours as I do). His need is for fairness.

Similarly, "I feel that you are lazy" is not a feeling, but a thought. The feeling is, "I feel tired and overwhelmed" (when you don't help do the dishes). The need is for support.

As a rule, when "I feel" is followed by "that" or by "you" it is generally not a feeling that is being expressed but a thought, assessment, conclusion, or judgment.

Watch out for conclusions concealed as feelings, such as "I feel abandoned" "I feel betrayed" or "I feel used." These statements all add a toxic charge of resentment, judgment, or conclusion.

"I feel abandoned" is more accurately expressed as the feeling "I feel sad and lonely" plus the thought "He left and is not coming back" or "I'll always be alone."

"I feel betrayed" is the feeling "I feel angry" and the thought "She didn't keep her promises."

"I feel used" is the feeling "I feel disappointed" plus the thought "It isn't fair."

"Clean" pain comes from dealing with the situation. "Dirty" pain comes from adding toxic layers of resentment, judgment, assessment or conclusion to "clean" pain.

The Peace Method® is a great tool to strip away the layers of "dirty" pain so that you can help yourself or your coaching client deal directly with the challenging situation. You look at each painful thought and investigate it to gain clarity.

One of the beautiful things about taking your time to tease apart feelings and thoughts, is that you will gain clarity on needs that are not being met. Then you can take action to get those needs met—or make a request that would get those needs met. This is the purpose of the final step of the Peace Method®.

Coaching is about helping our clients get their needs met. I'll talk more about needs a little later.

In the above example, the frustrated wife stated, "I feel I am living with a wall." With coaching, she realized that she feels lonely when her husband doesn't talk to her. After exploring the painful thought, "My husband shuts me out" and seeing some ways that she shuts her husband out, she could be enthusiastic about asking her husband for a "date night" once a week. She can also meet her need for greater connection by scheduling time with her friends.

COMMON HAPPY FEELINGS

- Affectionate
- Compassionate
- Confident
- Enthusiastic
- Energetic
- Fulfilled
- Glad
- Happy
- Hopeful
- Inspired
- Joyful
- Optimistic
- Peaceful
- Playful
- Proud
- Relieved
- Thankful

COMMON UNHAPPY FEELINGS

- Afraid
- Angry
- Ashamed
- Confused
- Despair
- Disappointed
- Discouraged
- Distressed
- Frustrated
- Helpless
- Hopeless
- Impatient
- Insecure
- Jealous
- Grief
- Guilty
- Lonely
- Heartbroken
- Miserable
- Overwhelmed
- Torn
- Sad
- Stressed
- Unhappy
- Upset
- Weary
- Worried
- Yearning

Painful Thoughts

As we conclude this discussion of the value of fully expressing your thoughts and feelings, I thought you would appreciate a list of some common painful thoughts. Circle the ones that seem true to you. Those would be great thoughts to take through the five-step Peace Method® process.

COMMON PAINFUL THOUGHTS

- I'm not good enough
- I need a partner
- I don't know what to do
- I need more money
- Life isn't fair
- I need to make a decision
- I can't do anything right
- It's my fault
- I missed my chance
- I failed
- S/he rejected me
- There's too much to do
- People are judging me
- I need to be in control
- He/she betrayed me
- He shouldn't be angry
- He/she did it wrong
- I am too old/young
- I am right
- Life is difficult
- It's too late

If everyone has these common painful thoughts from time to time, are these thoughts even yours? Can you remember the first time you had this thought? Was it actually <u>your</u> thought? Or was it something your mother or father or someone else said?

What if you are like a powerful radio receiver and you are picking up thoughts and feelings broadcast by others? What if there's nothing wrong with that—unless you claim the thought as yours? What if you could examine all your thoughts and just keep the ones that empower you?

CHAPTER 5

ACCEPT &
APPRECIATE

❧

Pain is physical, suffering is mental.
Suffering is due entirely to clinging or resisting.
It is a sign of our unwillingness to move, to flow with life.
Although all life has pain, a wise life is free of suffering.
A wise person is friendly with the inevitable and does not suffer.
Pain they know but it does not break them.
If they can, they do what is possible to restore balance.
If not, they let things take their course.
– Nisargadatta

The next step in the Peace Method® is acceptance. Resistance creates stress. Acceptance creates a world of possibilities. Resisting is like standing by a locked door trying to yank it open, shouting in frustration, "This door shouldn't be locked!"

Acceptance is like noticing that particular door is locked, and looking around and noticing that another door is wide open, a window is open.

Appreciation notices the beautiful garden, a puppy to play with, and a new friend.

Acceptance doesn't mean that we don't take action in the present to create a better future. As author Ram Dass put it so beautifully, "Compassion in action is paradoxical and mysterious…. It accepts that everything is happening exactly as it should, and works with full-hearted commitment to change."

Acceptance simply means that we stop making war with the present, stop wasting energy resisting the past. History never changes. Resisting shuts your mind and heart to a world of empowering reactions.

Peace comes when you accept things as they are, not as you wish that they were. You can wish for things to be different in the future, you can take action to create a better future, but in this moment, you need to accept things as they are.

If you have a thought about something that may happen in the future, you allow it. You don't need to accept it as real, as it hasn't happened yet. Making an allowance for that future possibility will reduce stress and invite wise choices.

Acceptance will change your life. When you accept the current situation, you release all victim energy.

Life is like the Japanese martial art Aikido. Aikido is performed by blending with the motion of the attacker and redirecting the force of the attack rather than blocking it. This requires very little physical strength as the practitioner uses the attacker's momentum to defeat him. A black-belt Aikido master will use this technique, and you can, too. In contrast, directly opposing the blow maximizes the force of impact, like two cars having a head-on collision.

Allowing the situation to be what it is frees you to focus on the actions and choices that are available, rather than draining your energy by "pushing against" reality.

As Deepak Chopra put it, "When you struggle against this moment, you're actually struggling against the entire universe." Struggling against the entire universe is a pointless waste of energy.

The wise understand that life has seasons. As it says in Ecclesiastes, "There is a time for everything, and a season for every activity under heaven; a time to be born and a time to die, a time to plant and a time to uproot, a time to kill and a time to heal, a time to tear down and a time to build, a time to weep and a time to laugh, a time to mourn and a time to dance."

After accepting the present, go deeper. Find something to appreciate.

Gratitude and appreciation are the keys to enjoying a fulfilling life. As we seek things to appreciate, it helps us shift to a better perspective. Whatever we focus on expands. Focusing on gratitude expands your awareness of blessings—and attracts more blessings into your life.

Appreciation is the fuel for creating a great life. The future is something you create by appreciating the present, and appreciating the possibilities for the future. Wasting energy resisting the past is like trying to drive looking only in the rear-view mirror. Ineffective — and you're likely to have an accident!

In his wonderful book *Peace is Every Breath* Thich Nhat Hanh writes, "If we can see and understand our own suffering, then we can easily see and understand the difficulties in another person, and vice versa. This is the practice of looking deeply into the first and second of the Four Noble Truths, the four sacred and wonderful truths in Buddhism. The Four Noble Truths are: first, there is suffering; second, there is a path or a series of conditions that has produced the suffering; third, suffering can be ended—happiness is always possible; and fourth, that there is a path that leads to the cessation of suffering, to happiness. Recognizing and acknowledging our difficulties (the first Noble Truth), then looking deeply into them and their root causes (the second truth), we are able to see the way out, the path of liberation (the fourth truth); the transformation and cessation of suffering accomplished by taking that path is the third Noble Truth."

Our work at the Grief Coach Academy is very much in alignment with Buddhist principles. We are devoted to helping people take the path that will lead to the cessation of suffering.

As an example of the life-changing power of acceptance, I'd like to share a dream I had on the second anniversary of David's death. This is an excerpt from my book *From Heartbreak to Happiness*.

ACCEPTANCE

I meet my dead husband at the airport. We sit across from each other, and I unleash my fury, How could you die beside me? How could you rip my heart out? How could you abandon me?

I pound my fist on the cold, hard, cheap table, heedless of the faceless passersby, all heading purposefully somewhere else. My fury spent, my voice quavers as I confront him with his ultimate betrayal, How could you leave our son without his father?

Silently, compassionately, my husband listens to the outpourings of my raging heart. He does not take the baited hook, nor does he reach out to comfort me with his warm, strong hands. He reaches out to me in the only way he can — in this dream.

If you had it to do all over again, would you still marry me?

I think for a moment, flooded with joyful memories. Love shared, boats sailed, dreams achieved — together. I'd take my time with him, though it be short. Yes.

If you had it to do all over again, would you still have our son?

This time the answer is quicker, surer. I wouldn't give up our son for the world! He is the light of my life, my joy, my blessing. Yes!

Given that, would you want to know that I would die young?

His question gives me pause. Would I choose to taint our joy with dread? I look into my heart, and after a long moment, see the answer. No.

A sense of peace soothes my rage and my sorrow. I did not choose my fate. And yet — I would.

Appreciation

Every cloud has a silver lining, if you're willing to look for it. Are you willing? Here are some questions to consider:

- What's right about this?
- What if something good is unfolding here?
- What can you appreciate about this situation?
- What can you appreciate about yourself or others?
- How does this situation serve you in some way?
- How does it help you grow?
- How does it deepen your compassion?
- How could this be an opportunity to change a pattern that doesn't serve you?
- Brainstorm one way you would willingly choose the present situation. (For example, if your other option was X, you would willingly choose the present situation. Find what X is for you.)
- What if there are no mistakes?
- What if you chose this situation before you were born?
- How could this situation propel you towards your Divine destiny?
- If this was your only path to enlightenment, would you choose it?
- If this was actually a gift from your higher self, how could it be a blessing?

Gratitude & Your Brain

When you bring your attention to the things you are grateful for in your life, your brain actually works better.
— Dr. Amen, author *Magnificent Mind at Any Age*

Dr. Amen and psychologist Noelle Nelson did a study on gratitude and appreciation. She had her brain scanned twice as research for her book *Power of Appreciation*. The first brain scan was after 30 minutes of meditating on all the things she was grateful for in her life.

Several days later, her brain was scanned again after she did a fear-based meditation. Her fearful brain looked very different from her grateful brain. Dr. Amen discovered that she had dramatically decreased activity in two areas of the brain: the cerebellum and the temporal lobes. When the cerebellum experiences low activity, people get confused more easily. They are less likely to think their way out of problems. They are clumsy and less coordinated. When the temporal lobes experience low activity, mood, memory, and temper control can be negatively affected.

Expressing gratitude on a regular basis will help you be healthier, and have a sense of well-being. Gratitude makes you more optimistic, which helps you make more progress towards your goals. Gratitude helps you think more clearly and will support you in problem-solving. Amazingly, gratitude will also help you perform better as an athlete.

Modern neuroscience tells us that our past reactions are engraved onto the synapses that send messages from one neuron to another, making them more likely to send the same message in the future. Much of our thinking is habitual. Why not train your mind to have the habit of thinking grateful thoughts?

Your Choice: Better or Bitter?

Whenever tragic loss occurs you either resist or you yield. Some people become bitter or deeply resentful. Others become compassionate, wise, loving. Yielding means inner acceptance of what is.
— Eckhart Tolle, author, *The Power of Now*

At the moment of crisis, when devastation hits, people face a life-changing choice: better or bitter? One choice is to sink into bitterness and resentment. The other choice is to open your heart and connect with the wise, compassionate, amazing, Divine being you truly are. It's a critical choice. It's a critical window.

This is why I'm so passionate about training certified From Heartbreak to Happiness® coaches, because people in crisis need support. Heartbroken people can teeter between better and bitter, and it is a life-changing choice.

With the right coaching, you're gently guided to become better. But if nobody cares, and no one asks the right questions, you can easily sink into despair and bitterness. But you can always choose again. Every crisis is an opportunity in disguise.

A heartbreaking situation (such as a death, a divorce, a bankruptcy, or a job loss) is devastating. It's as though life throws you a curve ball. But you know the great thing about balls? The harder you throw them onto the ground, the higher they bounce! And we are all like balls. You can bounce back.

But it's your choice if you bounce like a ball or if you splat like an egg. It's your choice. In my experience, two things create the elasticity to bounce: support and inner acceptance of what is.

In her book *The Gifts of Imperfection* Dr. Brene' Brown expands on this, sharing that the most common factors of resilient people are:

- They are resourceful and have good problem-solving skills
- They are more likely to seek help
- They hold the belief that they can do something that will help them to manage their feelings and to cope
- They have social support available to them
- They are connected with others, such as family or friends
- They are spiritual and recognize that we are all interconnected
- They cultivate hope, set realistic goals, and believe in themselves
- They practice critical awareness, disputing "not good enough" gremlins

- They feel their feelings and lean into the discomfort of hard emotions rather than avoiding or numbing out

The average child laughs hundreds of times a day. The average adult laughs only a dozen times a day. Norman Cousins literally laughed himself back to health, as he reported in his book *Anatomy of an Illness.*

Question: Why do angels fly?

Answer: Because they take themselves lightly.

Event + Reaction = Outcome (E + R = O)

It isn't life's events, but ones reactions to them that activates stress.
– David Hawkins, author *Power versus Force*

You cannot choose all the events in your life, but you <u>can</u> choose your reaction. Your reaction to events will amplify or minimize stress. A wiser reaction will produce a better outcome.

There is a little gap between what happens and how you react. The more peaceful you become, the bigger the gap. The bigger the gap, the more choice you have.

With most people, an event produces an automatic knee-jerk reaction. In truth, there is a tiny little gap between the event and your reaction. That gap is the opportunity for conscious choice.

Eventually, with practice, it becomes event, the sense of all the space in the world, and then a peaceful, conscious choice. A better reaction will produce a better outcome.

Are you reacting in the way that will give you the best outcome?

EVENT + VICTIM STORY = MISERY

An event plus a victim story leads to misery. If you're feeling like a victim at this moment, I can relate. I felt like a victim after my husband died. Don't make your feelings wrong. Breathe deeply. Bring your awareness into fully feeling your feelings in your body. What if every feeling fully felt turns into peace?

Every moment is an opportunity to choose again. What choice will produce the best possible outcome?

You may not choose the cards that are dealt to you, but you do choose how you play your hand. You can't necessarily choose every potential outcome, you're limited by the cards that you're dealt. But you still have a wide range of reactions you can choose. People might say, "Oh gosh, you got twos and threes and a five. How unlucky!" You might just play those cards and get a royal flush. Who knows?

Facing facts is always empowering. In my case, my husband died. That's a fact. I'll always be alone, that's a story. That's a theoretical projection of a future outcome. There's a big difference.

What you think creates your emotions. Staying with the facts will yield the best reaction and the best outcome. A painful story will create fear, panic, and stress. That emotional turmoil will trigger a poor reaction and then create a bad outcome.

This is why feeling peaceful is not a "nice to have" but a necessary strategy. When you're peaceful, you can think clearly. When you think calmly, you can choose a better reaction and create a better result.

But when you're freaking out, you catastrophize. Before you know it, in your mind, you're a bag lady and your children aren't speaking to you, and you're an alcoholic to boot. You get so far down into your nightmare, you can't think calmly. Your nightmare sabotages your ability to calmly and rationally deal with the one thing that is actually happening in the present moment that requires your response. Such as: how do I react to the fact that I lost my job?

Emotion is energy in motion. It can fuel action. It can guide you in the right direction. Pain can be powerful fuel to motivate productive problem-solving action, such as writing your resume and applying for jobs. Sometimes it's good to get disturbed, then get busy!

Emotion is a useful compass. It will tell you it you're going in the right direction. Follow the feeling of expansiveness, possibility, and lightness. If you follow this yellow brick road, it will lead you towards happiness.

Acceptance & Setting Goals

Whatever the present moment contains, accept it as if you had chosen it... Make it your friend and ally, not your enemy.
—Eckhart Tolle, author *Power of Now*

Acceptance does not mean being passive, having no goals, and taking no action. Acceptance means to observe "what is" — and not waste precious energy struggling against the present — then to wisely take right action peacefully and proactively.

The dictionary definition of "accept" includes: "to respond or answer affirmatively to" and "to undertake the responsibilities, duties, honors, etc. of." Your actions and goals are the way you respond to a situation, and the way that you undertake the responsibilities presented by the situation.

Accept the present and allow the future. The definition of "allow" includes: "to take into consideration" (as in allow an hour to change trains). When you take factors into consideration, you make wiser plans. For example, when you allow for an hour to change trains, you can change trains peacefully.

How can you more deeply accept the ebb and flow of the tides of life, without the need to make anything wrong? If you panic when the sun sets and night falls, you only add terror to the night; but the morning will dawn each day, right on schedule, regardless of whether you spent the night in terror or in peaceful slumber.

Acceptance and appreciation are like a candle you light at night. There is no need to fight the darkness. Instead, choose the light of conscious awareness. It only takes one flame to dispel the darkness.

The following questions can help you select fruitful actions and goals:

- How can you make the best of this?
- How does this situation invite you to redesign your life in constructive ways?
- What's the best possible outcome in 5 minutes?
- What actions can you take right now to create the best possible outcome in 5 minutes?
- What's the best possible outcome in 5 months?
- What actions can you take today to create the best possible outcome in 5 months?
- What's the best possible outcome in 5 years?
- What actions can you take this week to create the best possible outcome in 5 years?
- What else is possible?
- What state of mind will allow you to have clarity and ease around this?
- What have you been choosing not to see, know, learn, or receive about this, up until now?
- How could you have a breakthrough here?
- Will you choose peace instead of pain?
- How can it get better any than this?
- What possibilities are available now that you haven't yet chosen?
- What would you need to be, do, learn, or receive to make it better?
- Who has already succeeded who could help you?
- What actions can you take now to create a new and better reality?
- What reality are you fully capable of generating, creating and implementing?
- What do you consciously choose?
- What do you demand of yourself?
- Who can coach or mentor you?

- What can you learn to deal with this challenge more effectively?
- What have you already learned?
- How could that help others, save them time, money, or pain?
- How could helping others create prosperity or be a contribution?

As Zig Ziglar said, "You can have everything you want –if you help enough other people get what they want." Helping others overcome similar challenges once you have triumphed over them yourself is a recipe for happiness and prosperity. You might become a coach, consultant, mentor, speaker, or author and make an income as you make a difference. Or you may volunteer your time to help others. When you help others, you transmute the lead of a heavy heart into a golden gift to the world. It is alchemy.

Wisdom

Wisdom is knowing what to accept, and what to change. The Serenity prayer says so much in so few words. Having the wisdom to discern the difference between those things we can change and those things we can't change is essential for peace of mind.

THE SERENITY PRAYER

God grant me the serenity
To accept the things I cannot change;
Courage to change the things I can;
And the wisdom to know the difference.
– Reinhold Neibuhr

We can change ourselves. That takes courage and action. We can influence other people, but change is up to them.

A sure recipe for misery is to ignore the changes that you can make in your own life, while demanding that others conform to your expectations.

Some good questions to ask yourself include:

- Who does this belong to?
- Whose problem is this?
- Whose business is this?
- Who has the power to change this?
- Is this mine?
- Whose side of the street does this belong to?

You are empowered when you clean up your own side of the street.

I like Byron Katie's clarity. She's a spiritual teacher and the author of the wonderful book *Loving What Is*. Byron Katie says there are only three kinds of business in the world: my business, your business, and God's business (the God of your understanding).

When we are in someone else's business, we create a sense of loneliness and separation and angst. We're over there in their business—and they are over there in their business—and there is no one left here with us in our business.

Become aware of whose business you are in. Here are some examples. How would you answer these questions?

- Whose business is it if I am grieving because a loved one died? *My business*
- Whose business is it if you are worried because I'm grieving? *Your business*
- Whose business is it that people die? *God's business*
- Whose business is it if there is unemployment?
- Whose business is it if you are unemployed?
- Whose business is it if your son is unemployed?
- Whose business is it if your daughter is failing college?

- Whose business is it if you are paying for her college tuition?
- Whose business is it if your father remarries six months after your mother dies?
- Whose business is it if you are still grieving your mother's death?

Grieving people are often in someone else's business. They are over there in the grave with the dead person, in the dead person's business. There is no one left here with them.

Notice areas in your life where you are in someone else's business. Reclaim your serenity and power by choosing to stay in your own business.

Forgiveness

> *Forgiveness offers everything I want. What could you want that forgiveness cannot give? Do you want peace? Forgiveness offers it. Do you want happiness, a quiet mind, a sense of worth and beauty that transcends the world? ... All this forgiveness offers you, and more.*
> — *A Course in Miracles*

Forgiveness does not mean condoning or approving of the past. It means to let go of the past so you don't pollute the present with the past. Replace attack with acceptance. That is forgiveness.

Forgiveness is your ticket to freedom. It's something you do for yourself. Forgiveness is not about the other person. Forgiveness is about you.

When you are resentful, you have toxic emotional poison inside your body. When you are resentful, you are holding onto the past. You are spoiling this precious moment with the memory of something that happened in the past.

As the Chinese proverb says, "Holding onto resentment is like taking poison and waiting for the other person to die."

It's not the bite of the snake that kills you—it's the venom coursing through your veins. Resentment is the venom that kills your life.

The beginner level of forgiveness is giving up the hope for a different or better yesterday. You can do that. It's insane to think that yesterday is going to change.

At the mastery level of forgiveness, your resentment completely evaporates. Nothing is left but gratitude.

A Course in Miracles states, "Let me recognize the problem so it can be solved. Let me realize today that the problem is always some form of grievance that I would cherish.... The problem is a grievance; the solution is a miracle. And I invite the solution to come to me through my forgiveness of the grievance, and my welcome of the miracle that takes its place."

An elderly monk told his story of 20 years of imprisonment, torture, and isolation. The Dalai Lama asked him, "Was there any time you felt your life was truly in danger?" The old monk replied, "The only times I felt deeply endangered were the moments I felt in danger of losing my compassion for my jailers."

Forgiveness is an important topic beyond the scope of this book, and something we delve deeply into at the Grief Coach Academy with many different forgiveness processes. Let me give you one powerful and simple forgiveness process.

Hawaiian Forgiveness Prayer

When I interviewed Marci Shimoff, New York Times best-selling author of *Happy for No Reason* she shared an ancient Hawaiian Kahuna practice called Ho'o pono pono. It consists of silently saying four sentences while sending goodwill to anyone you are upset with.

I invite you to try this simple practice to free yourself of resentment. The four sentences are: "I'm sorry. Please forgive me. Thank you. I love you." You can say them in any order. It is a mental cleaning process.

Dr. Hew Len teaches this ancient Hawaiian forgiveness prayer. He says that you are thanking the Divine for cleaning and clearing your mind. You're cleaning the part of you that has the "program." If you didn't have the "virus," it wouldn't show up in your world, according to Dr. Hew Len. So, if anyone is annoying you, you clean and clear that same "fault" in yourself.

Dr. Hew Len believes in taking 200% responsibility for his world. He worked in the Hawaii State Hospital for the criminally insane. He believed the prisoners wouldn't be in his world unless he shared their issues. He didn't meet with the prisoners. He stayed in his office, looked at the files of the prisoners, and cleaned and cleared himself. In other words, if the prisoner was violent, Dr. Hew Len cleaned and cleared himself of any violent thoughts or actions by saying, "I'm sorry. Please forgive me. Thank you. I love you."

"I was simply healing the part of me that created them," said Dr. Hew Len.

In just four years, the hospital was transformed. Criminals were rehabilitated, released, and the ward was closed. For more information on this amazing story, read *Zero Limits* by Dr. Hew Len and Joe Vitale.

HO'O PONO PONO

I'm sorry.	*(For being unaware)*
Please forgive me.	*(I didn't know what I was creating)*
Thank you.	*(For taking care of this, God)*
I love you.	*(Reconnect to Divine love)*

"Turns out loving yourself if the greatest way to improve yourself, and as you improve yourself, you improve your world," Dr. Hew Len.

Now that we have explored the value of acceptance and appreciation, including the value of forgiveness, the next step in the Peace Method® is to consider the contrary.

CHAPTER 6

CONSIDER THE CONTRARY

ॐ

*We cannot solve our problems
with the same thinking
we used when we created them.*
—Albert Einstein

Challenging ourselves to consider the contrary is the fastest way I know to have quantum leaps of consciousness, clarity, and prosperity. We live in a world of duality—right or wrong, good or bad, black or white. When we challenge ourselves to see things not as "either/or" but as "both/and" we open a world of possibilities. In other words, when we consider that something is right <u>and</u> wrong, good <u>and</u> bad, black <u>and</u> white, we move beyond the trap of duality.

David Hawkins, author of *Power vs. Force* says that when we do that, we shift our level of consciousness to the 600s, which is the level of peace and the beginning of enlightenment.

Many spiritually-inspiring books, such as *A Course in Miracles* or the *Tao de Ching* invite us to pierce the veil of duality and see things with fresh eyes as "both/and" rather than "either/or."

When you challenge yourself to see if the contrary is true, a lightning bolt of insight can come in a flash. You can have a revelation that changes your perspective and your life.

I remember one of the most powerful times this happened in my life, which was in 1991, shortly after my husband died suddenly at the age of thirty-three. I went from knowing that my nightmares were the problem — to realizing that they were the solution. What a dramatic mind shift!

Here's what I wrote in my diary 100 days after my husband died. This diary entry was later published in my book *From Heartbreak to Happiness: An Intimate Diary of Healing*.

MAKE IT STOP!

Every night, when I lay my head down on the pillow, it's with dread. Every night is the same. I awake in the middle of the night from the same nightmare. Reliving every second of his death.

I can't sleep. I'm so tired. I look haggard. My clothes hang off me. I try drinking before bed and fret that I'll become an alcoholic.

Debara dismisses that worry, "Did you have a problem with drinking before?"

"Well, no."

"Don't worry about it. It's temporary," she says.

Still, a drink a night or even two is a lot for me, and an unfamiliar pattern. Besides, it doesn't work. I get homeopathic sleeping pills. But nothing takes a bite out of these nightmares.

His gasping breath. I turn on the light. His eyes are bulged, unseeing. "David, you're scaring me!" No response. I give CPR. He pees in the bed. Oh shit, oh shit, oh shit!

And I awake, drenched in sweat. I'm desperate. So here I am seeing a therapist for the first time in my life.

"So, what seems to be the problem?" the therapist asks.

"I'm having nightmares. You have to make them stop."

"What are the nightmares?"

"They're nightmares of my husband dying beside me. He died a few months ago. I can't sleep. You have to make them stop."

"Well, just a minute here. Tell me more about your life," the therapist insists.

I don't want to get bogged down with details. I don't want to get all emotional and cry. I want results.

"How are you during the day?" the therapist prods.

"The days are okay. It's the nights that are a problem." Make it stop, make it stop, you've got to make it stop!

"How are you getting through the day?" the therapist persists.

"Okay. I just pretend that my husband is away on a business trip, and then I can function. It's the nightmares I can't bear." Make it stop, make it stop, you've got to make it stop!

"So—you get through the day by pretending that your husband is away on a business trip?"

"That's right." It works. What's it to you?!

"Maybe your nightmares aren't the problem," says the therapist.

What!? *"What do you mean?"*

"You're not living in reality. Your husband isn't away on a business trip. He's dead. Every night when you go to sleep, your subconscious reminds you of that fact. Over and over, like clothes spinning in a dryer, your subconscious mind is telling you the truth."

But I can't bear the truth.

"You have to deal with the truth. The dreams aren't the problem. They're the solution. Getting through the day by living a lie is the problem."

Oh.

After this conversation, I saw my nightmares as a gift, calling me to deal with the truth. As I dealt with the truth, the nightmares stopped.

As I shared in my intimate diary of healing, many times quantum leaps in peace and healing came on the heels of considering the contrary. Here's another example from my book *From Heartbreak to Happiness*, this one written four years after my husband died.

WHAT IF?

What if the universe is not conspiring against me? What if it is actually supporting me – teaching me, leading me? What if it is working to make all my dreams come true?

The evidence – in the form of a series of unlikely coincidences – is mounting…. It seems that every time I go looking for something small, the universe hands me something bigger and better. What if I could trust that and relax into it?

What if everything is working out <u>exactly</u> as it is supposed to?

You Get to be Right

Whatever you think, you get to be right. Whatever we seek, we find. It pays to interrupt the habit of seeing things from a negative or painful point-of-view.

The biggest limitation is our own thinking. It is our "auto brake" mechanism that keeps us playing safe, playing small, and playing in our "comfort zone."

Here's another example from my book *From Heartbreak to Happiness*, this one written 181 days after my husband died.

ENERGY DOWNPOUR

My workout this morning is incredible! I feel like a playful colt surging with power and energy. I work out on the Stairmaster machine at level 12 (the maximum). In fact, I could push much harder, except that the machine's auto brake mechanism stops me. I'm not even panting. It's easy. Fun.

My mind revolts. "This is impossible! I can't keep this up." Immediately upon having that thought, it's true. I can't.

I realize that as much energy as I want is available — only my mind limits me. My mind is my personal "auto brake mechanism." I take the brake off — and the "impossible" is easy once again....

I work out for almost two hours. No matter what I do, it is easy. Level 8 on the rowing machine is no different from the Olympic level. If I tell myself that I'll do something, I accomplish it with ease.

Only our minds limit us. Revelation.

Guilt & Considering the Contrary

After coaching many people through grief, a clear pattern has emerged. Grieving people consistently search for some reason to blame themselves, especially for a sudden death. It doesn't matter that the reason is illogical. It is more bearable to crucify oneself than deal with the fact that we are not in control.

Guilt is the flypaper that keeps people stuck in grief. Considering the contrary is essential to releasing guilt.

Here's one more example of how considering the contrary changed my life. Six months after my husband died, I was crucifying myself with guilt. I visited a psychic, and she challenged me to consider the contrary. Here's what happened (excerpt from my book *From Heartbreak to Happiness: An Intimate Diary of Healing*):

THE PSYCHIC

Guilt turns and turns within me, like some green crocodile roiling inside me. Nastier than bile, gnawing on me from the inside.

I killed my husband. I knew I did! If only I'd been a better wife. If only I'd realized the stress he'd been under. If only we'd hired a mover. If only I'd known better CPR. If only the phone had been connected. If only I hadn't abandoned him to follow my dream of being a writer. If only I'd immediately spurned the flattering attentions of my mentor.

My mind seizes upon this last. That must have been the final blow. How could I accept all these well-meaning condolences when I knew I'd killed him?

An irregular heartbeat? That's no reason to die. This must be my fault.

I want to die. But that option is out. I'm not going to leave our son an orphan. But this guilt is unbearable. I need some relief. In desperation, I consult a psychic. ...

I share my anguish. Did I somehow cause David's death?

"You're not the center of the universe. His death isn't about you, it's about him. He had his own destiny, his own life — his own death," Fae says.

With trepidation, I blurt out my "infidelity."

She laughs at the absurdity. "A stolen kiss, a moment's confusion — that's not infidelity." She dismisses my earnest self-accusation and chides me to get a proper sense of perspective. "What protégé wouldn't be confused when her Mentor tells her he loves her? It happens on movie sets so frequently, it's cliché. The thrill of creating something together is mistaken for something else, when all it is about is the joy of creation and the sweet taste of success. You didn't have sex. It didn't go anywhere. You told him you loved your husband and your son and would never leave them. Let it go."

But my heart's crushing burden is not so easily dislodged. "How do I know David didn't leave this planet because he felt me leaving him?"

Fae smiles sagely. She challenges my perceptions. "How do you know you didn't feel attracted to your Mentor because you felt your husband leaving you?"

Prior to this session, it had never occurred to me that I might have felt a fleeting attraction to my mentor because I sensed that my husband was going to die. But once I was challenged to consider that, it felt true. In fact, it felt much truer than the opposite thought. After all, I had had a premonition of David's death. We were very connected and in tune with each other. David did the things he would have done, had he known he was going to die — he moved his family closer to family and friends the day before he died, he paid all the bills, he sold our business, he drafted his will, he spent time with his son.

Considering the contrary brought me peace of mind. It empowered me to resolve my grief and move forward. It can do the same for you.

Your Thoughts Are Real: They Change Your Brain, Your Body & Your Life

Your thoughts matter. In fact, your thoughts become matter.
—Dr. Joe Dispenza, author *Evolve Your Brain.*

I recently interviewed Dr. Joe Dispenza, the author of *Evolve Your Brain*. He shared the latest brain research. The way we think affects our body as well as our life. Your every thought produces a biochemical reaction in the brain. Every thought you think is matched by a chemical. Your thoughts become matter.

For example, when you think happy, inspiring or positive thoughts, your brain manufacturers chemicals (dopamine) that make you feel joyful, inspired, and uplifted. On the other hand, if you think unworthy, hateful, or angry thoughts, your brain produces chemicals (neuropeptides) and your body responds. You will feel unworthy, hateful, or angry.

The brain changes in response to every experience, every new thought, and every new thing we learn. This is called plasticity, which is the brain's ability to remold, reshape, and reorganize itself well into adult life. For decades, scientists thought that the brain did not generate new brain cells. Recent studies have shown that fully mature adult brains can produce additional nerve cells every day. In fact, the brain is continuously reorganizing itself.

Your thinking creates your state of being. This creates a self-reinforcing loop, unless it is interrupted. You begin to think the way you are feeling. And you being to feel the way you are thinking. Your automatic negative thoughts are like a computer software program running in the background of your life.

In my experience, automatic negative thoughts are not true. But they will continue to run your brain, body, and life unless you challenge them, and hold them up to the light of truth.

The good news is, you can elect to change the software program running your life. The bad news is, unless you challenge your negative thoughts, they will self-perpetuate and you will feel the way you are thinking. Even worse, the thoughts will tend to produce the outcome they fearfully anticipate.

Automatic Negative Thoughts

Thoughts are real and they have a real impact on how you feel and how you behave. Like a muscle, the thoughts that you exercise become stronger and become the thoughts you rely on, good or bad.... Every cell in your body is affected by every thought you have.

—Dr. Amen, author *Magnificent Mind At Any Age*

Dr. Daniel Amen is a clinical neuroscientist, psychiatrist, and brain imaging expert who heads up Amen Clinics.

Dr. Amen talks about the importance of liberating yourself from the lies polluting your brain. He teaches his patients ANT therapy—a way of challenging your Automatic Negative Thoughts (ANTs). Like ants at a picnic, the ANTs in your head can ruin your day. You do not need to believe every thought you have. Instead, confront negative thoughts with internal logic. You can learn to eliminate ANTs and replace them with positive thoughts that are true.

There are different kinds of ANTs, from blaming, labeling, fortune-telling, and "always/never" thinking. You can rid yourself of these pesky creatures by identifying them and crushing them with the truth.

Keep It Simple

Our minds operate much like a google search. Whatever we search for, we will find. It pays to interrupt a habit of seeing things in a negative way and look for how things might be positive. Only look for the contrary of painful, fearful, unhappy or stressful thoughts.

Considering the contrary works best if you change only one word at a time, and keep it very simple. For example, the contrary of "I am poor" is "I am not poor" or "I am wealthy."

What if the truth always makes you feel lighter and a lie always makes you feel heavier? Consider the contrary of thoughts that make you feel heavy, tight, or constricted.

Other Methods for Releasing Painful Thoughts: a Systematic Process Works Best

Painful thoughts are like individual bricks in the wall of a brick prison. On the other side of the brick wall is freedom and a beautiful garden. You don't have to remove all of the bricks in order to escape to freedom — you just need to create a big enough hole to slip through.

Just as if you were trying to escape a prison, you would focus on one brick at a time and see if you could loosen it or dislodge it. So methodically focus on one brick or one painful thought at a time. If you throw your shoulder against the entire brick wall of painful thoughts and limiting beliefs, you will just get a sore shoulder. But if you work on one brick at a time, you have the sure and steady path to freedom.

At the Grief Coach Academy we use many coaching processes in addition to the Peace Method® to help people go From Heartbreak to Happiness®.

There are many excellent processes that can help you explore painful thoughts and release them. A systematic process works best.

One process is the ABCDE process refined by Dr. Seligman, author of *Learned Optimism* based on the work of Dr. Ellis. It's a way to respond to adversity. A stands for Adversity, B for Belief, C for Consequence, D for Dispute and E for Energize. Adversity is the event that happens, belief is how the adversity is interpreted, and the consequence is the resulting feeling and action. Disputing negative beliefs is next, followed by energizing the desired outcome.

Byron Katie has a wonderful process called "the work" which involves four questions and a turnaround. The questions are: 1) Is it true? 2) Can you absolutely know that it's true? 3) How do you react when you believe that thought? 4) Who would you be without that thought? Then you turn it around, or look for how the opposite might be true. I highly recommend Byron Katie's books and seminars. She's a wise and inspiring spiritual leader.

The Sedona Method is another powerful releasing process. Hale Dwoskin, author of *The Sedona Method* is a friend and I've had the pleasure of interviewing him. The Sedona Method asks these questions: 1) Could you accept this thought? 2) Would you? 3) When?

NLP (Neuro-Linguistic Programming) and EFT (Emotional Freedom Technique) are other popular processes for releasing painful thoughts.

When I was editing this manuscript, I learned of another great process in Jack Kornfield's book *The Wise Heart*. He shares that Buddhist retreats for Westerners often teach the four principles for mindfulness transformation using the acronym RAIN: recognition, acceptance, investigation, and non-identification. Jack Kornfield writes, "The Zen poets tell us that "the rain falls equally on all things," and like the nourishment of outer rain, the inner principles of RAIN can transform our difficulties." Recognition is being willing to see what is really happening. Acceptance is the willingness to relax and open courageously to the facts. Investigation is to see deeply, considering body, feelings, mind, and dharma. Non-identification is to stop taking the experience as "me" or "mine."

The more I research, the more processes I discover! What this reveals to me is that people benefit from having a structured process to work through grief, stress, and other challenges. The above processes are additional resources you may wish to explore.

As you embrace empowering thoughts that will help you achieve your goals, it helps to remind yourself of past successes. Facts from your own experience are a powerful proof. As you discover evidence, your brain makes new connections and pathways. Finding evidence is like throwing wood onto a flame. Your new, empowering thought goes from a flickering candle flame to a blazing bonfire.

CHAPTER 7

ENTHUSIASM

&

All we need to make us really happy
is something to be enthusiastic about.
— Charles Kingsley

"Enthusiasm" is Latin for "in" + "God." So it means to be Divinely inspired, or filled with God.

Adults sometimes fall into the trap of thinking that they can't be enthusiastic when they are dealing with grief or a major crisis. If there is any time when it is absolutely essential to be filled with God's guiding inspiration, it would be when you're facing a life-changing crisis. It is not loyalty to the dearly departed to turn away from God, it is insanity.

Whatever God means to you, whatever faith you follow, having something to be filled with God about is like having a north star to guide you. Its light will be a beacon pulling you forward in the right direction.

Having something to be enthusiastic about is like having a rope thrown to you when you are mired in quicksand. Instead of focusing with panic on the quicksand about to engulf you—and thrashing about, which will only ensure your head goes under faster—enthusiasm calms the mind and invites productive action.

The dictionary definition of enthusiasm also includes: 1) absorbing or controlling possession of the mind by any interest or pursuit; lively interest: She showed marked enthusiasm for her studies. 2) an occupation, activity, or pursuit in which such interest is shown: Coaching is her latest enthusiasm.

This final step in the Peace Method® invites you to take your eyes off the problem and look to the solution. What do you consciously choose?

Focusing on the positive is ancient wisdom, as illustrated by this passage from the bible:

PHILIPPIANS 4:8

Finally, brothers, whatever is true,
whatever is noble, whatever is right,
whatever is pure, whatever is lovely,
whatever is admirable – if anything is excellent
or praiseworthy – think about such things.

The Enthusiasm of a Child

Living in a state of enthusiasm is the native wisdom of children. Fifty-five days after his father died, I took my son to Hawaii for a vacation with family. His enthusiasm is infectious. (Excerpt from my book *From Heartbreak to Happiness: An Intimate Diary of Healing*.)

A FIVE-YEAR-OLD ON LOVE

"I love you more than my new clothes or more than my video game or more than anything! I love you more than 'Flying Mario.' That's a hard-to-believe-one, isn't it?! I love you more than going on an airplane. Whoa! I love you more than this new house that we're living in now." (A condo in Hawaii.) *"I love you more than Santa Claus and more than presents. Whoa! Isn't that good?! I love you more than anything! I love you more than a star!"*

AURORA WINTER

"I love you more than that!" I protest. "I love you four million-billion-zillion. I love you like crazy wildfire. I have the galloping greedy gimmies of love for you! You are the light of my life, the joy of my joy, the happiness of my happiness!"

I tickle him, and he giggles happily.

"I love you with all my might. Say that on it, Mom." Yale points at my open journal.

I comply, writing it down.

"Read it to me."

I read it back to him.

"Write down, 'I love you' at the end of it," Yale says.

I do.

Yale says, "Love is an important thing. Write that down."

I do....

"I thought of another one!" Yale crows excitedly. "I love you more than my new fishing rod. That's hard to believe! And I love you more than my bow and arrow!"

Love is an important thing. I couldn't agree more.

Connecting with Enthusiasm

Here are some questions to help you connect with enthusiasm:

- What do you love doing?
- What do you love to have around you?
- Whom do you love?
- What goals would you love to accomplish?
- What activities bring you joy and fulfillment?
- What makes you feel important?
- What really matters in your life?
- What accomplishments are you proudest of?

- When does time fly?
- What are your core strengths?
- At your funeral, what would you love people to say about you?

Enthusiasm means there is a deep enjoyment in what you're doing, plus the added element of a goal or a vision that inspires you.

When you add a goal to the enjoyment of what you do, the energy field changes to a higher vibration. When your creative energy is fueled by enthusiasm, you will feel like an arrow that is swiftly moving towards your target—and enjoying the journey.

When your life is filled with enthusiasm, you can enter a period of time where you accomplish more in the next 12 months than you previously accomplished in 12 years. Author and entrepreneurial expert Dan Kennedy calls this "the phenomenon."

To an onlooker, it might appear that you're under stress. Stress only occurs when you're resisting what is, when you're not enjoying the present moment.

With enthusiasm, you are fully enjoying the present moment as you work towards creating the vision that you clearly see in your mind's eye.

Stress reduces the quality and quantity of your achievements. Stress is the area of struggle, striving and working hard to achieve your goals. Stress is fear.

With enthusiasm, you work with joy. Support comes to you from unexpected sources. You enjoy creative breakthroughs and achieve goals easily and effortlessly.

With enthusiasm, you don't have to do it all by yourself. You're supported.

Enthusiasm knows where it is going, but at the same time, it is deeply at one with the present moment, and so it is connected to the aliveness, joy, and power that are available only in the present moment.

To harness the power of enthusiasm, make sure your goals are connected to an activity, rather than an end result.

Focusing on the end result can trigger your ego and stress. (Examples: getting interviewed by Anderson Cooper, having a New York Times best-selling book, having a $1,000,000 annual income.)

Instead, enjoy the journey. Focus on inspiring people and contributing to their lives. That will keep you connected to enthusiasm, and will fuel joyful achievement with grace and ease.

Enthusiasm Creates Breakthroughs

When he was only nine, my son Yale got clarity on his dream of being a video game designer. This dream is still the "north star" of his life. He got a full-tuition scholarship to study game, art, and design. He graduated with a Bachelor of Science in game, art, and design. He has designed many games (check them out online at www.yalegames.com or www.skyisarrows.com) and now, at the age of twenty-six he is devoted to making his dream come true.

That's almost two decades of forward momentum, and I can trace it all back to fanning his enthusiasm when he was only nine. Here's what happened (excerpt from my book *From Heartbreak to Happiness®: An Intimate Diary of Healing*):

YALE'S BREAKTHROUGH

"My real dream is to design video games!" Yale says with conviction.

"Okay! Let's talk about making that happen." The more we talk, words tumbling out of both of us in an excited torrent of dream-making, the more his dream seems to grow from a fragile, tentative flame into a blazing bonfire.

We talk about how he can get started right now — keeping his mazes, reading video game magazines, making lists of things he thinks would be great in a game, learning more computer programs.

He's grinning from ear to ear. "Mom, I love future talk!"

Excited, Yale designs a computer animation with dollar bills falling from the sky. Then the words "In the future" slide across the monitor, followed by "we'll be rich!" Impressive.

Late that afternoon, we drive to LA to have Thanksgiving dinner with friends. Yale eagerly suggests, "Do you want to talk about business, Mom?"

So we talk some more, full of ideas about the future. We talk about how many games he could sell, how much they'd cost to make, whether I'd give him some money to help him get started, and how important it is to him that everyone working behind the counter is nice to the customers.

Yale glances at the dashboard clock. "We left at 5:01. Guess what time it is now, Mom?" It's 5:47. Yale's astonished by how the time just flew by. He looks so alight with his dream, his life.

In LA, Yale shares his dream with Janna, and the looking-at-the-floor, scuffing his feet shy little-boy energy is mixed with a new fire and pride. When Janna takes him seriously, all the shy little-boy energy drops away. Yale holds his head high.

At dinner, Yale contributes to the conversation smoothly, mastering the conversational tempo for the very first time. He makes eye contact and speaks confidently. His new attitude shouts out, "I know I'm valuable and you'll want to hear what I have to say!"

My heart overflows with the sweet pride and joy of witnessing Yale's transformation. What a difference a day can make. What a difference believing in someone and encouraging him to reach for his dreams can make.

Meeting Needs Tragically or Joyfully

In the above example, Yale's need to be heard, understood, respected, and encouraged were met. His big bold vision for his life met his needs for significance, creative self-expression, meaning and purpose. When needs are met constructively, people flourish.

The following graph reveals four quadrants of human behavior. Only one quadrant is ideal, quadrant 2, which is the upper right corner. In this quadrant, you are focusing on things that make you happy, as well as meeting your needs. In quadrant 2, you're happy and productive. That's where enthusiasm lives.

4 QUADRANTS OF MEETING NEEDS

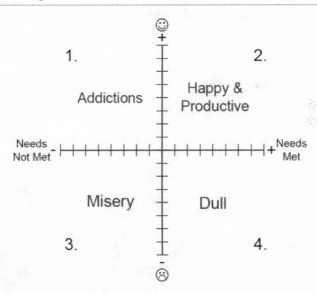

In quadrant 1, the upper left corner, you're focusing on things that make you feel happy—but at the expense of meeting your needs. This is the area of addictions—from shopping addictions to drug, alcohol or sex addictions. For example, someone who just lost their job and smokes pot to avoid the pain while not taking any action to find a new job is in quadrant 1.

In quadrant 3, the lower left corner, you are not meeting your needs or doing anything to produce happiness. You feel miserable. This would be the case of a grieving person who can't get out of bed, or someone who has just lost their job who obsesses about how things went wrong but doesn't take any action to find a new job or any action to cheer themselves up. Simple actions like seeing a movie or reaching out to friends can move you out of this miserable quadrant.

In quadrant 4, the lower right corner, you are meeting your needs, but not proactively doing anything to bring happiness, fulfillment or joy. This is the "life of quiet desperation" that Thoreau wrote about. This would be the case of our fired friend grabbing a job that barely pays the rent, but that doesn't allow him to express his core strengths, such as a creative person working in a warehouse.

By becoming aware of things that bring happiness, you can move from quadrant 4 to quadrant 2. For example, adding mediation, exercise, time with friends, gratitude, and a proactive search for a more fulfilling job, you could easily move to quadrant 2, so you would experience being happy and productive. Your life situation hasn't changed (yet), but your experience of your situation has dramatically altered.

If your top needs are being met, you will feel content and peaceful. If your needs are not being met, you will feel stressed and off-balance.

For example, a young widow may notice that her needs for: touch, physical affection, and caring are not being met since her husband died. She could chose to meet these needs by scheduling a weekly massage, getting a facial, getting a pedicure and foot massage, and getting weekly coaching support.

All people have needs. What are your top needs? Circle your top needs on this list.

COMMON NEEDS

Acknowledgement	Meaning
Appreciation	Mourning
Authenticity	Movement
Awareness	Passion
Beauty	Peace
Being Heard	Play
Choice	Protection
Comfort	Reflection
Contribution	Respect
Creativity	Rest
Family	Safety
Food	Self-worth
Freedom	Sex
Friendship	Shelter
Goals	Stability
Growth	Support
Healing	Teaching
Honesty	Touch
Independence	Trust
Individuality	Understanding
Love	Warmth/Caring
Mastery	Water

If your top needs are being met, you will feel content and peaceful. If your needs are not being met, you will feel stressed and off-balance.

What actions can you take to ensure that your top needs are met? What are some new ways to meet your needs? How could you design your life to meet your needs automatically?

What needs of yours are not being met right now? What actions could you take to design your life to meet all your top needs?

To learn how to communicate your needs to others effectively and constructively, read *Non-violent Communication* by Marshall Rosenburg. I had the pleasure of taking a nine-day workshop lead by Marshall Rosenburg, and highly recommend his work.

Anthony Robbins, author of *Unleash the Giant Within* says there are six fundamental human needs: the need for certainty, variety, love or connection, significance, growth and contribution.

I invite you to focus on fulfilling your needs for growth and contribution. Paradoxically, helping others is the fastest way to help yourself. I think George Bernard Shaw captured it best.

CONTRIBUTION

This is the true joy in life: The being used for a purpose
Recognized by yourself as a mighty one. The being a force
of nature, instead of a feverish, selfish little clod of ailments
and grievances complaining that the world will not devote
itself to making you happy. I am of the opinion that my life
belongs to the whole community, and as long as I live, it is
my privilege to do for it whatever I can.
– George Bernard Shaw

ENTHUSIASM = FORWARD MOMENTUM!

The final step of the Peace Method® invites you to take action on the insight and wisdom you have gained. Insight without action won't change your life.

Take some action, no matter how small, immediately upon completing the Peace Method® process and gaining clarity. This will gradually transform your life.

Now that we have looked at each step of the Peace Method® in depth, let's look at some actual examples of using it as a coaching process with real people just like you.

CHAPTER 8

REAL-LIFE
EXAMPLES

∂⌒

Example moves the world more than doctrine.
– Henry Miller

I'd like to acknowledge my students and clients, whose trust and willingness to grow makes my mission so fulfilling. I hope this book communicates some of the joy, pride, and gratitude I feel as I watch them transform their lives, relationships, and happiness. I'm in awe as they release their own grief—and then reach out to help others.

All the theory in the world is not as illuminating as some real-life examples. So that you can use the Peace Method® more effectively in your own life or as a coaching tool, here are some examples.

Many are transcribed from Grief Coach Academy coach training events or group training calls. Some are examples from my own life. Others are summaries of the essence of a coaching call or conversation, as best as I can recall. Names and other details have been changed to protect the privacy of my clients and students, and the content has been edited for clarity and brevity. The following represents the essence of actual sessions with real people.

"I have not been focusing on the ones I love"

Agatha is a baby-boomer, a caring mother, a respected professional, and a coach attending a Grief Coach Academy training event. Agatha is distraught and grieving because her aunt died last night. Her grief is fresh. She regrets that she missed the chance to talk to her aunt one last time. Agatha's response to her aunt's death is a normal reaction. In fact, it is almost a "textbook" grief reaction, so it provides a great example to study. After Agatha shares her grief and distress, she accepts my invitation to come onto the stage and receive coaching support. I begin by bringing her into the present moment with a brief meditation inspired by Thich Nhat Hanh, a Buddhist monk.

Aurora: (meditation) Inhale and relax your body, exhale and smile. Inhale coming fully into the present moment, and exhale knowing that it's a wonderful moment. Inhale and relax your body, exhale and smile. Inhale coming fully into the present moment. Exhale knowing that it's a wonderful moment.

So, I honor and acknowledge that the Divine is, it is the "I am that I am." It is that peace that surpasses all understanding. It is all needs met with grace and with ease. I honor and acknowledge that the Divine is in everything and in everyone, including in me, and including in Agatha. So I invite that part of us that is Divine or that part of us that's an instrument or channel for the Divine to be fully present right here and right now.

I invite in those quantum leaps of consciousness, clarity and peace of mind. I dedicate our time together to Agatha, and to whatever is in her highest and best good. That both now and later upon reflection, this time together will serve as a powerful catalyst bringing her greater wisdom, greater enlightenment, greater peace of mind. I release this intention with gratitude and with thanksgiving, because I know it was already done even before I spoke. So be it, and so it is.

Agatha: That helped already, actually.

Aurora: I'm glad.

Agatha: I am upset because I didn't call my Aunt Kathy and she died last evening. I should have called her after my cousin John sent me the information on her nursing home. I should be more aware of what is important to me. I need to focus more on those I love and less on what I have to do.

Aurora: What is most painful of all of those thoughts?

Agatha: I think what's the most painful is that I knew she didn't have a lot of time, but I just got so caught up in what I had to do. I didn't make the call, and it would have been easy to call. She was important to me. She gave me a lot of love.

Aurora: Yes. Take a deep breath. Another deep breath. I want to acknowledge that tears can just be love overflowing. I really honor the depth of your love for her. Grief can be like a storm, awesome even in the drama of the tears and the wind, a miracle in a way.

What's more painful for you: "she died" or "I should have called"?

Agatha: Well, she was 90 and not in good health. I think probably for her it was a blessing that she died. It's more painful for me that I didn't connect with her first. I think what's most painful is that I haven't been more focused on the ones I love and my extended family.

Aurora: All right, sweetheart, take a deep breath. Would you be willing to look at this one brick at a time, using the Peace Method®?

Agatha: Yes.

Aurora: Good. "I haven't been focusing on the ones I love and my extended family," is that about the past, present, or the future?

Agatha: It's present.

Aurora: Okay. Good, the present is your point of power. So, how do you react when you believe the thought "I haven't been focusing on the ones I love and my extended family"?

Agatha: (grieving) I feel sad. I feel I have all the time in the world to connect or reconnect, and I don't.

Aurora: Take a deep breath. How do you treat yourself with this thought, "I haven't been focusing on the ones I love and my extended family"?

Agatha: I've been beating myself up pretty bad.

Aurora: I can see that. What if it wasn't possible for you to believe that thought anymore: "I haven't been there for those I love"? Without that thought, who would you be right now?

Agatha: I'd be a lot more peaceful.

Aurora: Peaceful sounds good. So, the cost of this thought is your peace.

Agatha: Right.

Aurora: Any other feelings come up when you believe the thought "I have not been focusing on the ones I love and my extended family"?

Agatha: There's a little bit of panic because I do have a lot that's important to me that I'm doing in my life. Like, "My God, how do I do it all in a way that feels really good and I feel good about myself"?

Aurora: So, I'm going to write that thought down because that would be actually a good one to look at later, "how do I do it all and feel good with all my priorities." Let's continue looking at "I haven't been focusing on the ones I love and my extended family." Any other thoughts or feelings or reactions that come up when you believe that thought?

Agatha: Determination. I know I can. This has been a wakeup call.

Aurora: Nice wisdom. So, what I'm hearing is that you are allowing the thought, "I haven't been focusing on the ones I love and my extended family" and looking at it as useful information, like a wakeup call.

Agatha: Yes. I had an intuition a couple of weeks ago that I needed to be refocusing my priorities. I was thinking of in terms of my golden Rolodex®, the number of people who are important to me that I haven't been in connection with. But I kind of shut that voice off and got back to work.

Aurora: Could you just allow that and accept that as useful information?

Agatha: Yes. My intuition works pretty well when I listen to it.

Aurora: Good to know. So, what could you possibly appreciate about the thought "I haven't been focusing on the ones I love and my extended family"?

Agatha: Well, one thing that I could appreciate is that I do have a priority there that I've not been paying attention to.

Aurora: Until now?

Agatha: Yes, until now. I can appreciate it happened here actually [at a Grief Coach Academy coach training event, where she could get immediate support and coaching].

Aurora: Yes. That's true. That's a good point.

Agatha: (aware of the irony) Even though when I walked in [to the Grief Coach Academy meeting room] and I could feel I was about to start sobbing, I was ready to walk right back out. I thought, "No, this is not the place I should be breaking down."

Aurora: (laughs) That's funny. If not here, where? Anything else you'd like to appreciate?

Agatha: (smiles) I appreciate myself for all the times I have been there for my family and friends.

Aurora: Yes, absolutely. Well, let's look at that then. So, let's look at the contrary, "I have been focusing on the ones I love and my extended family." Tell me one time when you did focus on the ones you love.

Agatha: Well, I've been spending quite an amount of time supporting a friend whose grandson just committed suicide about two weeks ago. We drove to be with her at the funeral and support her family. I was able to offer support to her other grandson. Two of the three boys in that family have committed suicide. A lot of people were putting it on the third grandson, "We're so worried about you." So, I reassured him that he's not his brother.

Aurora: I get chills. You saved him from the people Velcro®-ing that projection onto to him. That was quite time-expensive for you. But you did it. You drove there. You were at the funeral. You supported various people. Sounds like you really have been there for the people you love.

Agatha: (nods) My sister's cancer has come back and I have really tried to be there for her.

Aurora: Did you send her a two-minute e-mail or...?

Agatha: No. I called her.

Aurora: Yes, you call her. So you're really there for your sister. Tell me more about how you have been focusing on the ones that you love.

Agatha: Really, my focus is on my husband and my children.

Aurora: You love them, they count. You went on that nice trip to Europe. Do you think they'll have memories forever from that?

Agatha: Yes. My eldest is so appreciative of the fact that he's really struggled to make a living following his passion, and gets a lot of messages why he should just make money. We've really supported him in following his passion. Now he finally has found a way to do that. He's so appreciative that we didn't give up on him or urge him to go the more accepted route.

Aurora: Yes. Well, that sounds life-changing and self-esteem changing. What I'm hearing from you is that you <u>are</u> there for the ones that you love.

Agatha: When I was thinking this morning of my sister, I had really judged her boyfriend because he's not faithful to her, and it caused my sister a lot of pain. I think I judged her, too. But he's the one who takes her to all her chemotherapy appointments every day and he gets her shots at night. I thought, "What a true friend. How can I ever judge that kind of love?"

Aurora: I'm hearing that you had a change of perspective about him. Isn't that a way that you are focusing on the ones you love — your sister and her husband — by extending that love, acceptance and forgiveness to him and choosing to see him in a different light? Isn't that an extension of love?

Agatha: Yes.

Aurora: (lightly) Yes. Well, I'd like to be in your extended family.

Agatha: You are in my extended family!

Aurora: Hallelujah! I know you focus on the people in your extended family.

Agatha: But you haven't even gotten an e-mail from me.

Aurora: I don't like e-mails, you know that about me. So, thank you for not sending me any. What I'm hearing from you is that you have been focusing on the ones you love. Is that true?

Agatha: True.

Aurora: Truth, which is more true, "I have been focusing on the ones I love," or "I haven't"?

Agatha: I have is more true.

Aurora: Absolutely.

Agatha: I have a huge family, so it's kind of hard.

Aurora: Who is the most important person to love so that you can support your enormous extended family?

Agatha: Me.

Aurora: Right.

Agatha: I started beating myself up so hard and so fast last night. I lost a lot of perspective.

Aurora: Well, you're gaining it back now, and then some.

Agatha: (hopeful) Yes. The other thing that comes to me is I really believe in my heart that I can still connect with my Aunt Kathy. I'm not very good at that though. So, it's being more aware on the spiritual level how I can connect with her and that I can still tell her how much I love her.

Aurora: Absolutely.

Agatha: (with regret) That maybe I missed the chance that I had.

Aurora: So, those are some other thoughts we could explore: "I missed my chance" or "I can't connect very well" we could look at that. Let's finish following this painful thought all the way through first.

What are you enthusiastic about choosing now given the insight you've discovered? Any decisions that come out of this?

Agatha: Definitely. When I plan my day, I have a to-do list. I go through — fix the car, get my eye appointment, work on my book, my coaching calls, all the appointments that I have. But I have not added as part of my to-do list specifically connecting with those I love. So I'm going to make that a daily to-do, to look at that every day and reach out in some way to support the people in my extended family.

Aurora: I celebrate that. That sounds very wise.

Agatha: Thank you.

Aurora: You're welcome.

"I missed my chance"

The above coaching session continues.

Aurora: Do you want to look at "I missed my chance"?

Agatha: (grieving) I don't know.

Aurora: Take a deep breath.

Agatha: (crying) God, I'm sorry, I didn't realize I had so much pain around that.

Aurora: Would you like to have less?

Agatha: Yes. But I feel like I'm taking too much of your time.

Aurora: (to attendees) Are you appreciating her authenticity and willingness?

Crowd: (murmurs of love and support) Yes! We're sending our love in plentiful measure.

Agatha: (to attendees) Thank you guys.

Staff: The live streamers are wrapping their arms around you. Eight, nine, ten comments…

Aurora: Take as much time as you need, sweetheart.

Agatha: Thank you. Okay, we'll try this.

Aurora: Okay, let's do another little meditation to come fully into the present moment. Inhale and relax your body. Exhale and smile. Help is on the way. So, inhale and relax your body, exhale and smile. Inhale coming fully into the present moment, and exhale knowing that it's a wonderful moment. Again, inhale and relax, exhale and smile. Inhale coming fully into the present moment, and exhale knowing that it's a wonderful moment.

As we honor and acknowledge that the Divine is, it is the "I am that I am," it is that peace that surpasses all understanding, it is all needs met with grace and with ease. I honor and acknowledge that the Divine is in everything and in everyone, including in me and including in Agatha. I invite in that part of us that is Divine, or that part of us that's an instrument or a channel for the Divine, so that we may be both be blessed with Divinely-inspired insight, wisdom, revelation, clarity and peace of mind.

I dedicate this time together to Agatha and to whatever is in her highest and best good, that both during our time together and later upon reflection this time together will serve as a powerful catalyst bringing her greater enlightenment, wisdom, clarity, happiness, joy and peace of mind. I release this intention with gratitude and with thanksgiving. So be it and so it is.

(pause)

So, "I missed my chance" — past, present or future?

Agatha: I guess it's past.

Aurora: One thing I know about the past: we can never change it. We can only accept it, and forgive ourselves and others. So how do you feel when you think the thought "I missed my chance"?

Agatha: Sad.

Aurora: How does the sad show up in your body?

Agatha: Like I just want to crawl up I guess.

Aurora: You want to crawl up?

Agatha: Yes. I feel really little.

96

Aurora: Whose business are you in with the thought "I missed my chance" — God's business, your business, Aunt Kathy's business?

Agatha: I don't know.

Aurora: That's good, the "don't know" mind is an open mind. Just consider the possibility that there are no mistakes. What if it's God's business whether you said hello to her last night or whether you say hello to her today?

Agatha: Okay.

Aurora: Does it feel lighter or heavier to think of it as God's business?

Agatha: It feels lighter.

Aurora: What if the truth always feels lighter? What if it wasn't possible for you to believe the thought "I missed my chance"?

Agatha: If I felt I could just happily and joyfully and instantly connect, I would feel really happy.

Aurora: Good. So would you be willing to allow this thought "I missed my chance" and allow the situation that your Aunt Kathy passed last night, without it being an attack? But like, "Oh, useful information, she's on the other side now." Could you just take a deep breath, and without making war on it just allow that she's dead or her body is dead. Take a deep breath. Pain is part of life, suffering is optional.

Agatha: Let's see if we can work on the suffering.

Aurora: Yes.

Agatha: I see it, I know it is God's business. I don't want the people around me to die.

Aurora: You want them to suffer?

Agatha: (laughing) No, I don't want them to suffer.

Aurora: All right. You were suffering a minute ago. But you're laughing now. Did your aunt suffer? Did she suffer last night?

Agatha: I don't know if she suffered last night.

Aurora: Is she suffering now?

Agatha: No, I don't think so.

Aurora: There you go, wish granted, people around you not suffering. It's good to appreciate the situation.

Agatha: I want it all my way. I want it in my time.

Aurora: I want it my way, my schedule. I love you for that. Let's look at the contrary, what's the opposite of "I missed my chance"?

Agatha: That I haven't missed my chance.

Aurora: Tell me how that's so.

Agatha: I do believe we're all connected and that she lives still, beyond it all, and that I can still send her love, and because we have had a loving connection that she still would feel that and be supported by that, whatever her experience is now. I just need to drop the fact that I'm not very good at connecting with people who died.

Aurora: Baloney.

Agatha: I even saw during Ho'oponopono that connecting was within me, like I wanted her forgiveness for holding that belief because it stops me from connecting. It stops me from sending love and reaching out.

Aurora: What is your point of view, people who are on the other side, do you think they're vibrating at 75 or 600? [referring to Dr. Hawkin's chart of consciousness, with 75 representing grief and 600 representing peace]

Agatha: My belief system is that they're vibrating at what they were vibrating when they passed over.

Aurora: Do you think they stay that way?

Agatha: No, I think growth is eternal.

Aurora: All right. How was your connection with her when she was alive? It was good?

Agatha: We had a loving connection.

Aurora: Your love is 500? [referring to Dr. Hawkin's chart of consciousness, with 500 representing love]

Agatha: Yes.

Aurora: Tell me more about "I <u>didn't</u> miss my chance."

Agatha: Well, I think it's only because I believe that I missed my chance; that I missed my chance. When I'm looking at "I didn't do this, I didn't do that when she was alive when I could have, and if I'd only reached out this week" instead of "I can connect, I can send her love, I can still feel that loving connection between us. I can send her gratitude for all the love she gave me."

If I'm not focused on "I missed my chance," I could focus on I have a chance every day, every minute. I have a chance to send love to her, instead of wasting my time with regret.

Aurora: A very wise woman.

Agatha: "I missed my chance" is not even true.

Aurora: Right. So what do you consciously choose now? Or what are you enthusiastic about given this wisdom?

Agatha: I'm enthusiastic about sending her my love and my gratitude, and my best wishes for where she is and what's she's experiencing. My love for her is as strong and my support for her is unwavering, even though she is dead, which is not mine to choose or change.

Aurora: Who would want that burden anyway if you were God and had all the choices?

Agatha: That's true.

Aurora: How are you feeling now?

Agatha: I'm feeling so much better.

Aurora: Good.

Agatha: I'm feeling like I can go ahead and participate [in the rest of the coach training event], not run and hide and beat up on myself.

Aurora: We don't want that. So, what I'm hearing from you is that it would be meaningful to you to connect. What I would love to offer is that we could all do the loving-kindness meditation and send your aunt Kathy loving-kindness, as well as you, and that we could lift up your intention to connect with the extra love and support of everybody here in person and attending via live streaming. Would you like that?

Agatha: I would love that.

Aurora: Okay, let's us do that. Take a deep breath. I'm going to send the Buddhist loving-kindness meditation first to you, and then to your aunt Kathy.

(to audience) Please join me in supporting Agatha with your loving energy.

(to Agatha) May you be filled with loving-kindness. May you be safe from inner and outer dangers. May you be healthy in body and mind. May you be at ease and happy. May you be filled with loving-kindness. May you be safe from inner and outer dangers. May you be healthy in body and mind. May you be at ease and happy.

(to her deceased aunt Kathy) Kathy, may you be filled with loving-kindness. May you be safe from inner and outer dangers. May you be healthy in body and mind. May you be at ease and happy. May be you filled with loving-kindness. May you be safe from inner and outer dangers. May you be healthy in body and mind. May you be at ease and happy.

(to Agatha) What words would you like to add to Kathy?

Agatha: (to her deceased aunt, voice strong and steady) Kathy, I love you, I thank you. What I'm remembering most strongly is when I was little, after my dad died, I was feeling so lost and so confused. I felt your loving support. I could be a child, I didn't have to have it all figured out at your house. I felt safe in your house and with your family. I felt that always with you, that you loved me just as I was.

I so appreciate the support that you gave. It was an oasis in my childhood, and sometimes I really needed that. I hope now that you see in review of your life all the love reflected back to you that you gave so openheartedly to others. I know you didn't have much in terms of material goods, but you sure made up for it in terms of the abundance with which you gave love and acceptance to those around you.

I hope you're experiencing now just the greatest happiness and the greatest joy, and that you're connecting with my grandparents and all those who've passed who love you, and that they're able to help you find your way in this new place where you are now. I hope they can give to you the comfort that you gave to me as a child. I love you so much. Thank you so much.

Aurora: (closing meditation) May you be filled with loving-kindness. May you be safe from inner and outer dangers. May you be healthy in body and mind. May you be at ease and happy.

Please take some deep cleansing breaths. When you're ready, come back in the here and now.

(pause)

How are you doing? You look a lot better.

Agatha: Thank you, I'm doing a lot better. Thank you for supporting me, I really felt your love and support.

Aurora: You're welcome.

Agatha: I just want to say thank you all for loving and supporting me through this, I really could feel it up here. It meant a lot me, it made it possible for me to do it. Thank you. Thank you, Aurora.

Aurora: You're welcome, sweetheart.

Grief is a normal and natural response to loss. Emotions can be intense. Yet with coaching and the opportunity for completion and closure, grief can pass quickly, like a summer thundershower. The next day can be bright and fresh like after a storm, smelling of flowers.

In this instance, Agatha was herself again the next day — cheerful and peaceful. Her grief had given her the perfume of a deeper wisdom, and a fresh appreciation for life and all its blessings.

I called her a week later, and she shared that the benefit of this coaching session remained with her. She felt complete with her aunt's passing, and was deeply grateful that she had had the opportunity to express her love and appreciation, and say goodbye.

"I don't know how to deal with it"

Ted is a kind, sensitive man in anguish over the suicide of his high school friend Peter some years ago. A student at the Grief Coach Academy, Ted has worked through many of his losses. He is ready to come to terms with Peter's death now.

Ted: I am angry, frustrated and sad with Peter, who was a classmate of mine because he committed suicide. I feel abandoned. This is something that happened just maybe a year or two before the ten-year high school reunion. It pretty much blew me out of the water and of course I did like most men did back then—I stuffed it. I just recently started to come to terms with it, but I don't know. Some days, it's okay and then other days, I don't feel complete on it.

Aurora: What did you want Peter to do?

Ted: Peter should have continued living and called me. Peter should have sought professional help or at least contacted me. It's frustrating because I don't know how to deal with it. It was just something out of the blue. He's the first—no, the second person outside of my family that I have lost in such a tragic death. That's like the second within about five years.

Aurora: Tell me about Ted.

Ted: He was very competitive. We played sports together. We were competing against each other. We were teammates. I know he was rather temperamental, but he also had a great sense of humor. We had good chemistry between us, so when he passed it just really shocked me more than anything else. It was totally unexpected. I had not known that he had any particular problems. After we got out of college we drifted apart, but it was just shocking to read that in the paper.

Aurora: Thank you for sharing. I would love to do the Peace Method® with you, if you're willing.

Ted: Sure.

Aurora: Let's see if we can find just one painful thought to take through this simple five-step process. We can't go back and help Ted in the past, but we can deal with what's happening to you right now. What thought is most troublesome to you today: It came out of the blue? He should have continued living? I don't know how to deal with it? He should have sought professional help? He should have contacted me? He shouldn't have committed suicide?

Ted: It always comes back to I didn't know how deal with it. I don't know how to deal with it now. I feel incomplete.

Aurora: You don't know how to deal with it. Let's look at that thought, then.
I invite you to come fully into the present moment, Ted, so that you can benefit from this simple process. Would that be all right with you?

Ted: Yes.

Aurora: So let's come fully into the present moment. I'll lead us in a little centering meditation, but please breathe at your own pace.
(meditation inspired by Thich Nhat Hanh) Inhale and relax your body, exhale and smile, inhale coming fully into the present moment, and exhale knowing that it's a wonderful moment. And again: inhale and relax your body, exhale and smile, inhale coming fully into the present moment, and exhale knowing that it's a wonderful moment.

So, Ted would it be all right with you if we focus our attention on just this one painful thought, "I don't know how to deal with it" and do the Peace Method® on that one thought?

Ted: Yes.

Aurora: If other painful thoughts come up, we'll write them down, but in order for you get the benefit from the simple process we'll agree to focus all the way through on just this one thought. If we change horses mid-stream, we'll just get muddy and wet, and we'll lose the benefit of this simple process. Okay?

Ted: Yes.

Aurora: So "I don't know how to deal with it"—is that a thought about the past, the present or the future?

Ted: Definitely present.

Aurora: How do you feel when you believe the thought "I don't know how to deal with it"? What happens?

Ted: I feel lonely and abandoned.

Aurora: Okay, and your body?

Ted: A feeling of scared, fear, like my body is tightening up, especially in the chest area.

Aurora: How do you treat Peter in your mind when you believe the thought "I don't know how to deal with it"?

Ted: I can't find the words. Like he's at a distance and it's like I'm reaching for him and can't touch him.

Aurora: And where did this thought "I don't know how to deal with it" first occur to you?

Ted: When I read the newspaper article.

Aurora: What else comes up for you when you believe the thought "I don't know how to deal with it"?

Ted: Confused at what's the next step. What do I do? You know how do I feel even? I was shocked and then somewhat numbed when I first got the news.

Aurora: Okay. So whose business are you in mentally when you believe the thought "I don't know how to deal with it"? Byron Katie [author of *Loving What Is*] taught me that there are three kinds of business: your business, my business and God's business.

When we are in other people's business or when we're in God's business we always feel lonely and separated and confused. For example, if you're thinking about Peter's suicide you're over there in the grave with Peter and he's over there in the grave with Peter and that leaves nobody here with you, Ted. We create loneliness when we are in other people's business.

So whose business are you in, Ted?

Ted: I'm in his business.

Aurora: And that's not wrong, but just to notice. Becoming consciously aware is a wonderful thing. So does this thought, "I don't know how to deal with it" bring peace or stress into your life?

Ted: Stress.

Aurora: I hear that. If it was no longer possible for you to believe the thought "I don't know how to deal with it" how would you be?

Ted: Strong, powerful, myself, my true self.

Aurora: Wow, that sounds good!

Ted: (excited) Yeah, as you were saying that it just clicked all of a sudden and went oh; oh and now I'm really starting to feel a different energy!

Aurora: Actually all my hairs are standing on end. I can feel the energy flowing through. Something shifted there in a wonderful way. Anything else you want to share about that before we move onto the next step?

Ted: I definitely feel a greater sense of empowerment in seeing that. I may have gotten ahead of myself, but when I heard the negative something clicked in me that said try the positive, and as soon as I did that it was like I could breathe — this big gasp of air came into me and just filled my entire body with a different energy.

Aurora: Great! So what I'm hearing is that you considered "I <u>do</u> know how to deal with it." Is that right?

Ted: Yes.

Aurora: Tell me about that, one way that you do know how to deal with it.

Ted: I feel it's time to let him go fully. I felt I had a partial release. I was writing about this a few months ago, and I did come to some peace with it, but I felt so incomplete. And now I'm ready to do that complete forgiveness, and that is pretty powerful.

Aurora: Very powerful and very wise. Ready to let him go fully. And I hear that you're ready to fully forgive?

Ted: Yes.

Aurora: Yourself probably as well as him?

Ted: Yes.

Aurora: So you really <u>do</u> know how to deal with this. That's what I'm learning from you.

Ted: Maybe I—I feel sometimes I have to give a voice to it. With this Peace Method® it's the method in which I could do this and something resonated within my heart and soul with this whole thing and it just allowed it to happen. I feel like I'm finally speaking my truth on this, getting more in integrity with myself.

Aurora: You <u>do</u> know how to deal with it.

Ted: Mm-hmm.

Aurora: You're dealing with it by speaking your truth. You're dealing with it by giving voice to it. You do know how to deal with it because you know it's time to let him go fully and you do know how to deal with it because you're noticing that it's time for a deep and complete forgiveness. This is great wisdom.

Ted: This is pretty powerful.

Aurora: I agree.

Ted: I think just I can be with that. I'm very comfortable with that.

Aurora: It's beautiful and wise and deep, profound and true. This has been such a huge and beautiful shift. It's such an honor to be a catalyst for you doing this wonderful work.

Do you notice anything that you are enthusiastic about? Or filled with God about? Or a conscious choice that you're ready to make now?

Ted: I had a lot of judgments around his actions. I was raised Catholic, so I had to deal with that stuff too. What I'm getting right now is that I can let him go in peace.

Aurora: That sounds like something to be enthusiastic about.

Ted: Yeah.

Aurora: Does that feel like the truth?

Ted: Yes, very much.

Aurora: Wow, that's deep. Good work Ted.

Ted: Thank you. Now I'm feeling all this energy.

Aurora: Yeah, I can feel it too. That thought "I don't know how to deal with it" was like a stopper on a champagne bottle and now that it's been freed, I sense your bubbly energy.

Ted: Mm-hmm.

Aurora: So how do you feel on a scale of one to ten with one being terrible and ten being great on this issue of "I don't know how to deal with it"? When we began and now?

Ted: I think it varied from a minus three to a plus three at the beginning, and now my cup runneth over. Wow, that's a big wow, yeah; definitely I'd say ten, maybe more. I'm feeling much better, just wow, feeling things I haven't felt in a long time about myself.

Aurora: Good. It set you free. You just set yourself free.

Ted: Definitely.

Aurora: And you've already done many things to deal with it, including writing your book, including enrolling at the Grief Coach Academy and now you're aware that it's time to let him go fully.

Ted: Mm-hmm.

Aurora: And you're speaking your truth. There's a resonance in your voice. Can you hear it?

Ted: Yes, I can definitely feel it.

Aurora: Yeah, it's powerful. I'm excited. You're going to be a force to be reckoned with, with your book and speaking and coaching now that your voice has been freed. Watch out, world!

Ted: I'm really amazed. Just my own experience is like wow. It's an "aha" moment.

Aurora: And now you have a deep knowing that you can give this gift to others because you embody it. Right?

Ted: Mm-hmm, definitely! Thank you.

Aurora: You're welcome.

There are a couple of things I want to point out from this coaching session. Neutral curiosity is the coach's ideal attitude. Ted was dealing with heavy grief, so I met his energy where it was, and slowed my pace to match his.

When Ted jumped ahead to consider the contrary, I followed his lead. We skipped over the A, the accept and appreciation step. If he hadn't gotten an enormous release, I would have circled back around to explore acceptance and appreciation.

Enthusiasm means to be filled with God, and I shared that definition with Ted to make it seem more appropriate. In my experience, it's a beautiful thing to be enthusiastic about letting somebody go in peace, or to consciously choose to let somebody go in peace.

"He's not a good provider"

Petra is a young widow who recently remarried. Her second husband is a musician, and Petra is frustrated with his lack of financial success. In this session, I coach her through a painful thought as I demonstrate the five steps of the Peace Method® during a group training call at the Grief Coach Academy.

Petra: I'm frustrated and disappointed with my husband because he's not as successful as I'd like him to be. Dan and I got married a year ago. He should lose weight and he should spend more time on his projects and he should watch what he eats. I love him dearly and I think he's an amazing man and I know we're soul mates, but this part...it puts a space in between us as far as I'm concerned.

Aurora: Tell me more about Dan.

Petra: He is passionate. He's a talented musician. He is a hard worker, very sensitive and positive. He's content with what he has and doesn't have the drive to make more money. He needs to be more successful.

Aurora: How successful should he be?

Petra: He should have enough money in the bank for us to have our own place. We're right now living with my mom. He's living paycheck to paycheck and he's doing his own thing and I'm doing my own thing and I don't like that. I want us to support each other. And of course I have the conversation in the back of my head that the man needs to bring money, not the woman. He's not a good provider.

Aurora: Let's do the Peace Method® on this thought "he's not a good provider." Would that work for you?

Petra: Yes, of course.

Aurora: In order to get the benefit of this simple process we'll stick to the thought "he's not a good provider" and we'll follow it all the way through. Just as if you were actually trying to escape a prison and you were trying to loosen a brick so that you could escape. If you just loosened a little bit of 15 different bricks you're not going to get your freedom, but if you focus on one brick at a time, you can loosen it, or pop it out, and make more headway escaping the brick prison that way. So let's agree that we'll focus on this one brick "he's not a good provider." Does that work for you?

Petra: That sounds good.

Aurora: All right, so now let's come into the present moment with a few deep, cleansing breaths. Inhale and relax your body, exhale and smile, inhale coming fully into the present moment, and exhale knowing that it's a wonderful moment.

Our bodies cannot tell the difference between a problem in our mind or a problem in the present moment. So I'm curious. Is this thought "he's not a good provider" a thought about the present, the past or the future? And there is no wrong or right answer.

Petra: Let's see. Well this was in my space even before we got married and it hasn't changed. I think it's from the past.

Aurora: Good to notice. What I know is that we can never change the past. We can only forgive and let go. So I invite you to notice that.

Petra: Okay.

Aurora: So the next step with the Peace Method® is to express your feelings. In my experience, it's very important that we have the opportunity to fully express all of our feelings so that we can release them, especially the feelings that we wish we didn't have.

Petra: Yeah, exactly.

Aurora: So when you have this thought "he's not a good provider" how do you feel Petra? What happens?

Petra: He becomes someone that I can't rely on.

Aurora: "He's someone I can't rely on" is another painful thought you could do this process on. Coming back to this one brick with the thought "he's not a good provider" what emotions do you notice when you have the thought "he's not a good provider"?

Petra: I get frustrated. I feel it in my upper body through my chest area. I feel sad and unfulfilled, like I made a mistake marrying him.

Aurora: So, "I made a mistake."

Petra: That's another thought, huh?

Aurora: Right. That's another thought. I'm going to circle that. This is actually wonderful that these other painful thoughts come up. It's juicy. You're noticing that in fact there are some other painful thoughts adjacent to the brick called "he's not a good provider." It would be great for you to do the Peace Method® on "I can't rely on him" and on "I made a mistake." The beauty here is that if you release a few bricks you may have a big enough hole to escape the entire brick prison! So this is wonderful. So Petra, how do you treat your husband when you believe the thought "he's not a good provider"?

Petra: I don't treat him very well. I want to nag at him and I want to complain. I try not to, but I know I put him down.

Aurora: Good to notice.

Petra: Yeah, and I blame him.

Aurora: Good to bring that into your conscious awareness. How do you treat yourself when you have this thought "he's not a good provider"?

Petra: I blame myself. I don't trust. I don't trust my intuition and it's not a good place to be. That's for sure. I don't like being there.

Aurora: Whose business are you in mentally when you believe the thought "he's not a good provider"? Your business, his business or God's business?

Petra: Definitely his business.

Aurora: Good to notice. And does this thought "he's not a good provider" bring peace or stress into your life?

Petra: Just stress!

Aurora: All right, anything else you'd like to share around how you feel with the thought "he's not a good provider" before we move onto the next step?

Petra: There is fear about the future. I worry what if I settled, what if I made a mistake?

Aurora: This thought definitely brings stress. I hear that.

Petra: Yeah, yeah.

Aurora: Okay, so let's continue to focus on the one thought "he's not a good provider" right now. Take a deep breath.
So, in my experience it's just a thought. I'm curious if it might be possible for you to accept that sometimes that's true? That

sometimes "he's not a good provider" might be a true statement from time to time? Would you be willing to accept that without making yourself wrong, without making him wrong, but just as a neutral observation?

Just notice "oh, today he's not a good provider" just like you might look out the window and notice "oh, it's raining today" without it having anything to do with how beautiful the world is and the fact that there still definitely is blue sky behind the clouds. Could you allow this thought "he's not a good provider" without having to make war with it?

Petra: I'm trying to accept it, but it brings sadness because I don't want that to be between us. But I like what you're saying, that you can look out the window and there is sky and there are beautiful flowers, but...

Aurora: Well, here's what I'm inviting you to do. I'm inviting you to notice that it might be true on a specific day, but that doesn't have to be his identity.

Petra: I see.

Aurora: So there is a gap there. To allow what is. What happened today is: it's a rainy day. What happened today is: he's not a good provider today. It doesn't have to be his identity forever.

Petra: (excited) Oh my God. Yes, I can do that! Thank you!

Aurora: Good work. So what if this is actually a gift from your higher self? How could it possibly be a blessing?

Petra: That he's not a good provider?

Aurora: How could this situation or this thought be a blessing?

Petra: It could be a blessing. So I would get on the ball and I would empower him to really see who he really is. He is a powerful man and he can do anything.

Aurora: And do you think that will go better if you're holding it as a momentary thing? As opposed to his identity being "he's not a good provider" versus oh, just on this particular day maybe he wasn't as good a provider as possible? Which way do you think will go better?

Petra: Yeah, definitely that would work much better if I think of it as a temporary thing.

Aurora: Just like when it's raining you know it's definitely raining and yet you also know that the blue sky is behind the clouds. You know that Dan is this amazing, passionate, talented, hard-working, sensitive, positive man. That's who he truly is.

Petra: Yes, that's great! Thank you, Aurora.

Aurora: You're welcome, Petra. Continuing the weather metaphor, every cloud has a silver lining if you are willing to look for it. Are you willing?

Petra: Yes, I am.

Aurora: So what could there possibly be to appreciate about this situation? What could you appreciate about the thought "he's not a good provider" or appreciate about the situation that your financial goals are not yet met?

Petra: I can think about how we can create this part of our lives together.

Aurora: Good.

Petra: I feel so much better!

Aurora: I'm happy to hear that you're feeling better. So when we started this how were you feeling on a scale of one to ten? With one being really crappy and ten being really great on the issue of "he's not a good provider." How were you feeling at the start and how are you feeling now?

Petra: I was like three and now I'm more like eight or nine on a scale of one to ten. I feel much lighter.

Aurora: I'm so glad to hear that, Petra. What if the truth always makes you feel lighter?

Petra: I like that.

Aurora: In my experience, we suffer when we don't see the whole truth and all of the possibilities. So would you be willing to consider some other possibilities?

Petra: Yes, of course.

Aurora: Okay. So what is the contrary or opposite of "he's not a good provider"?

Petra: He is a good provider.

Aurora: Okay, tell me about that.

Petra: He's very supportive of me and my dreams. If I need anything, he is there 100%.

Aurora: Nice.

Petra: Yeah, he's really great.

Aurora: Tell me more about "he is a good provider."

Petra: He's great with my family. He loves my sisters and just he loves the get-togethers. I'm from Iran, so it's a different language that's being spoken when we get together, but he doesn't mind. He gives me a lot of support, and assistance. He has my back.

Aurora: He has your back. Well that's pretty good! He's supportive of your dreams. He's 100% there if you need something. He's great with your family. He loves your sisters. He's agreeable even though a different language is being spoken. Basically bottom line is, he's got your back.

Petra: Yeah.

Aurora: Given that evidence, would you say that "he is a good provider" is a true statement?

Petra: Yes.

Aurora: Is it as true or truer than "he's not a good provider"?

Petra: I think it's truer.

Aurora: Great.

Petra: Yeah, definitely truer.

Aurora: So the final step of the Peace Method® is enthusiasm. All we really need to make life worthwhile is something to be enthusiastic about. So given this wisdom that you've discovered through these simple questions, what are you enthusiastic about being or doing with your husband?

Petra: Enjoying our time together, really enjoying each other and celebrating what we have because we found each other, we were meant to be together. Celebration, celebration of our love and togetherness. It's really great.

Aurora: Okay, so that's the Peace Method®. The five steps are: P: present moment, E: express your feelings, A: accept and/or appreciate, C: consider the contrary, and E: end on enthusiasm. So Petra, what's your overall experience?

Petra: Wow, I really feel light, open. The sadness is gone and I feel like I can actually put this aside and not look at it again, and if I do, I know it's going to be just for today. It's kind of hard to explain. I feel an openness that wasn't there before. I can give him more space to be successful. I know that he couldn't be successful in the way I was looking at him before.

Aurora: Now you've got an openness that can be an invitation for him to expand into?

Petra: Yes!

Aurora: How are you feeling now on a scale of one to ten?

Petra: I'm a ten.

Aurora: You're a ten?

Petra: Yes.

Aurora: How nice is that!

Petra: That was great! Thank you.

Aurora: You're welcome.

This is a nice, clear example of how using this simple process and taking your time exploring each of the five steps with your coaching client can bring insight, clarity, and joy in less than 30 minutes.

"I didn't get to say goodbye"

Susan is a middle-aged government employee who came home from work to discover her husband's dead body. She was agonizing over not getting to say goodbye to him. Here's the essence our coaching call, which took place about two months after her husband died.

Susan: I just can't bear it that I didn't get to say goodbye. And now it's too late. It's so awful.

Aurora: Would you like to do the Peace Method® with me on "I didn't get to say goodbye"?

Susan: Yes.

Aurora: (after a brief meditation to bring Susan into the present moment). So, I'm curious, is this thought "I didn't get to say goodbye" about the past, the present or the future?

Susan: The past.

Aurora: Okay, good to notice. And what I know about the past is that we can never change it. No matter how much we think it should have been different. Your only point of power is the present moment.

Susan: (sad) Yeah, well in the present moment I'm miserable because he's dead and I didn't get to say goodbye.

Aurora: (reassuring) I understand. That's grief. What else comes up for you when you think the thought "I didn't get to say goodbye"?

Susan: Kind of spinning in my head. Going over and over and over that day. I should have come home earlier, I should have known. I feel like a bad wife. My heart hurts. It feels like there's a lead weight on it.

Aurora: Mm hmm. It's a heavy thought. Would you be willing to just allow space for that thought, without crucifying yourself with it? So that "I didn't get to say goodbye" is more of a neutral observation?

Susan: I could try.

Aurora: Good. Take a deep breath, allow that in. In my experience we suffer when we don't see the whole truth and all the possibilities. Would you be willing to consider some other possibilities?

Susan: Yeah.

Aurora: Would you be willing to consider the contrary of "I didn't get to say goodbye"? What's the exact opposite?

Susan: I did get to say goodbye?

Aurora: Yes. How could "I did get to say goodbye" be true?

Susan: (thinks for a moment) Well, I kissed his forehead before I left for work. He was sleeping. That's kind of a goodbye. (pause) And I whispered "bye" when I left our bedroom.

Aurora: Nice. How else did you say "goodbye"?

Susan: Well, I called him from work on my lunch break. He didn't pick up, but I told him "I love you."

Aurora: Sweet. How else did you say "goodbye"?

Susan: (pause) Well, he was sick for a long time. We knew this day would come. We talked about it. I said my goodbyes then.

Aurora: So…what I'm hearing from you is that you kissed him goodbye. And you said goodbye when you left for work. You called him and told him you loved him. And you talked about it, and said your goodbyes. That's a lot of saying goodbye!

Susan: (laughing, having a mind shift) It is, isn't it?!

Aurora: Is "I didn't get to say goodbye" even true?

Susan: (overjoyed) No. No, it's not!

Aurora: Good to notice. You _did_ say goodbye.

Susan: Yeah. I did.

Aurora: Given this insight, what are you enthusiastic about doing or being now?

Susan: (happy) Letting that go. And spreading his ashes from a plane. He'd like that. And having a party to send him off in style. Invite our friends and relatives.

Aurora: That sounds great. Anything else you're enthusiastic about?

Susan: You know, now that I see what a big deal saying goodbye is, maybe I'll help other people organize celebration of life parties. So they can say goodbye to their loved ones. I'm good at organizing and it would feel great to contribute in this way, in his memory.

Aurora: Good idea! I love it….

(The coaching call continued and we brainstormed her new ideas. She had shifted from grief to enthusiasm.)

This was a life-changing moment for Susan. She was eager to release her grief and work through it. When she first began coaching with me, she self-tested as being in the least happy 15% of the US population. At work, her coworkers avoided her in the lunch room as she seemed to be in a black cloud of gloom.

Within just two months of coaching, her happiness increased dramatically. Using that same quick quiz, she was now above average in happiness compared to the US population. Her coworkers went from avoiding her to actively seeking her company. She told me that they were amazed by the transformation and wanted to know what her "happiness coach" (as she fondly referred to me) had been telling her. They wanted some more happiness, too!

Within a year, Susan was bubbly and enthusiastic about life. She said she was happier than she had ever been. She began dating, and found a wonderful man who adored her. A year later, she shared that she still treasured this coaching session and the resulting mind shift was permanent. She was grateful for how coaching helped her to rebuild a life filled with joy and meaning.

"I am going to die"

My 81-year-old father, George Winter, came to visit me in California. On a beautiful sunny day, we went for a hike in the Topanga mountains. Unlike me, my father is an atheist. He's a professor, an intellectual, a scientist, a skeptic, and an author. He has a great sense of humor and a warm, playful nature. My father has three children from his first wife, and two teenaged children from his much-younger second wife. On this walk, the fate of his young family was weighing heavily on his mind as he confronted his own mortality. This is the essence of our conversation, as best as we both can recall it. He gave me permission to share this.

George: When I was 70, I felt pretty good. Still pretty vibrant and strong. But these past ten years, I've really aged. My hearing is going. My eyesight is failing. I go to my son's hockey games but I can barely see them on the ice. I'm going to die. That's a heavy thought. From dust to dust.

Aurora: Would you like some support?

George: Sure.

Aurora: Would you be willing to do a five-step coaching process called the Peace Method®? It's basically five questions.

George: Sure, why not?

Aurora: How it works is we focus on just one painful thought at a time, and take it through this five-step process. It's a process of inquiry or discovery. There are no wrong or right answers. We're looking to discover what's true for you.

George: What's true is that I'm going to die. And there is still so much to do. My kids will grow up without me.

Aurora: Would you be willing to look at "I'm going to die"?

Frank: Okay.

Aurora: Is that a thought about the past, the present or the future?

George: Clearly the future.

Aurora: Good to notice. When we are anticipating the future, we miss out on the present.

George: True.

Aurora: What thoughts or feelings come up when you think the thought "I'm going to die"?

George: All the things I didn't do. I had so much promise as a young man. So many things I planned to do, but didn't get accomplished. So many things I still want to do.

Aurora: And so many things you did accomplish, too. You wrote two books, taught, travelled the world!
　　　　What else comes up you think the thought "I'm going to die"?

George: I want to finish my book and I don't know if I can get it done. I worry about my kids. They're going to grow up without their father. I don't want to be a burden. I'd rather die than be ill and need someone to take care of me.

Aurora: That's a lot.

George: Yes, but it feels good to share. It's a relief.

Aurora: I'm here for you. Any time. The next step in the Peace Method® is to see if you would be willing to simply accept the thought "I'm going to die." Perhaps it is just useful information?

George: I can accept it. It is useful information, actually.

Aurora: In what way?

George: To make the best of the time I have left. Surprisingly, that does feel a lot better. More peaceful.

Aurora: Peaceful is good. The next step is to consider the contrary. Just look at the opposite and explore if there is any truth to it.

George: The opposite of "I'm going to die"?

Aurora: Right. What's the opposite?

George: I'm <u>not</u> going to die.

Aurora: How could that be true?

George: It's not. I <u>am</u> going to die.

Aurora: I get that. We are all going to die. But just for a moment, would you be willing to see if there is any way that "I am not going to die" is true?

George: (thinks for a moment) I guess my DNA. My DNA will live on in my children. Not hugely comforting, but true.

Aurora: Any other ways that "I am not going to die" is true?

George: (thinks for a moment) I guess what I have taught my children will live on.

Aurora: (grins) I can attest to that!

George: (mildly) Doesn't change the fact that I am going to die. I don't believe in God or souls or the hereafter. I don't see things the same way you do. When I die, I'll return to dust. That's it.

Aurora: As I said, there are no wrong or right answers. It's about what's true for you. The final step of the Peace Method® is to ask, given the insight you've gained, what do you consciously choose?

George: (laughs) Well, I'm not dead yet, so I choose to make the best of it! I choose to spend time with my kids and people I love.
     I choose to enjoy this beautiful day with you.

Aurora: That sounds good to me, Dad. Feel any better?

George: You know, I do. Accepting the thought was surprisingly helpful and powerful. And it's good to talk about it, instead of ignoring the "elephant in the room." Thanks.

Aurora: I love you.

George: I love you, too. Pretty good process you got there. You should write a book about it.

Aurora: (laughs) Good idea, Dad!

I wanted to share this example because it shows how you can use the Peace Method® in a conversation with a friend or family member. I hope it also reassures you not to be afraid to talk about very painful thoughts or thoughts that may not have a valid contrary for that person. My father found great relief expressing his feelings. He had no one else that he could talk to about death so openly. So never underestimate the value of being willing to listen with compassion and caring.

In his book *How to be Compassionate* the Dalai Lama talks about the value of confronting our own mortality. "Accepting old age and death as part of life is crucial to making life meaningful.... Even for those who do not believe in future lifetimes, contemplation of the reality of impermanence is productive, helpful, and even scientific."

"I need her to stop criticizing me"

Lynn is a young widow grieving the recent death of her husband in a car accident. Lynn is struggling with life balance and the responsibilities of suddenly being a single Mom to four busy teenagers. Lynn's mother wants Lynn to take better care of herself. Lynn wants her mother to be more understanding and stop being so critical.

Lynn: I am disappointed at my mother because she told me I looked haggard and rundown in an email yesterday.

Aurora: Ow!

Lynn: Yeah. She should mind her own business. I need her to realize I'm one person doing the job of two people. I went to my daughter's track meet which took 12 hours, and then I went to her prom and took pictures, which was another four hours. But I'm one person and my mother's like, "Oh, my God, the picture of you looks so bad and haggard and rundown. What are you doing to yourself?"

I just need her to be supportive and appreciate that I'm doing the job of two people. I don't have anybody that can go sit at a track meet for 12 hours and do the stuff that a parent does. When you have two parents, it is easier. But I'm doing it by myself, so I think she should appreciate that I'm doing the best I can.

Aurora: Yeah, it takes a lot to be a single mom.

Lynn: She comes on so strong with these comments, like "you look so haggard." But my Mom is 85 and she doesn't really get it right now.

Aurora: Thank you for sharing, Lynn. Would you like to play with "I need her to stop criticizing me"?

Lynn: Sure.

Aurora: Let's take some deep, cleansing breaths together and come fully into the present moment, alright, Lynn?

Lynn: Yeah.

Aurora: I'll lead us in it, but breathe at your own pace. (deep breathing meditation)

So, Lynn, I'm curious. Is this thought, "I need her to stop criticizing me" about the past, the present, or the future?

Lynn: The present. Well, it's happened in the past, too. It's a common theme, let's say that.

Aurora: It's a common theme, okay. We can never change the past, but we can take action in the present. What comes up for you with the thought "I need her to stop criticizing me"?

Lynn: I just want her to understand more. I don't need her saying I look haggard. I know I shouldn't even listen to it. I know in my heart of hearts that she means well. But I don't want to hear that after I've just spent 14 hours at a track meet and a prom, and I don't have another person to share that responsibility with. And my parents are in Florida so they're not here, they can't say "oh, we'll do the prom." We don't have any other relatives here. It's up to me. Sometimes yes, I do look haggard and I am exhausted. You know, it's been a very busy weekend.

Aurora: A lot on your plate.

Lynn: Yeah. And I just want them to understand better, as they sit there in Florida. I did say, well, do you have any suggestions? Like who else was going to go to my daughter's regional track meet and the last one of her high school career? I was going to be there even if it meant sitting out there 13 hours.

Aurora: You're a good mom.

Lynn: Yeah. And I did look awful at the end of the day. It was the truth. I was literally exhausted. I had a flood in my house the night before, and it's like why don't you understand that my water heater burst, the relief valve burst, and I had a huge flood. And I had to drive to the airport in Boston to pick somebody up and driving in the car four hours on a Friday night. And then at 7:00 Saturday morning I jumped in my car to drive three more hours.

Aurora: Oh my, you're a trooper.

Lynn: Yeah. But, you know, it's just mothers; mothers are like that.

Aurora: So how do you treat your mother with the thought "I need her to stop criticizing me"?

Lynn: How do I treat her?

Aurora: Uh huh.

Lynn: I should say something to her but I just back off and I say oh, she means well. She wants me to look nice or look prettier. She keeps telling me to put blush on. I get where she's coming from. My mother is a very beautiful woman who cares about her appearance, and she always looks wonderful and is dressed to a T. And sometimes I'm just too tired to worry about stuff like that.

Aurora: You're very beautiful as well. So whose business are you in mentally when you believe the thought "I need her to stop criticizing me"?

Lynn: Her business because what other people think of me is none of my business.

Aurora: Exactly right.

Lynn: I totally get that.

Aurora: Yeah. Imagine it's no longer possible for you to believe the thought "I need her to stop criticizing me." How would you be right now?

Lynn: I would be peaceful because I would say it doesn't matter what she says. I'm just going to let it roll off my shoulders, and I'm not going to let it get to me, and I'm not going to think bad thoughts. I'm just going to let it go and she can say all she wants.

Aurora: That sounds peaceful. Anything else? Any other thoughts or feelings you'd like to share before we move on to the next step?

Lynn: No, that's good.

Aurora: Okay. Every cloud has a silver lining if you're willing to look for it. Are you willing?

Lynn: Yeah.

Aurora: Okay. So could you accept that your mother does criticize you and just allow that without making a war on it? Just notice, like you might notice that she's wearing a red dress? Knowing that it's got nothing to do with you?

Lynn: Yeah. I could if I didn't let the anger charge come through. I definitely could try that and let that be. I need to not be so reactive.

Aurora: Yes. Everybody's going to be reactive when they're tired as you were after that long day. That's the number one key to happiness — getting enough sleep! You can also allow yourself some room on that, and be kind to you. So what I'm hearing from you is that you could accept that sometimes your mother is critical?

Lynn: Yeah.

Aurora: Good. It happens sometimes. I'd like to invite you to share what you appreciate about your mother or about this situation.

Lynn: Well, I think she's wonderful and she loves me, and I know she only has my best interests at heart. She's trying to say to me, take care of yourself, which I need to do. Do more things for yourself, do less for your kids. I know she loves me. She's trying to watch out for me in her own 84-year-old way. So that's all good. And I'm really criticizing her criticizing me, so I'm doing the same thing back at her.

Aurora: Well, that's very wise, very insightful. So now that you've noticed that you're criticizing her criticizing you, how could this be an opportunity to change a pattern that doesn't serve you?

Lynn: Well, I just have to flip a switch and shift, and not react to it.

Aurora: (laughs) "Shift happens."

Lynn: Shift happens, and I just have to shift.

Aurora: I invite you to be gentle with yourself and say "I choose to" rather than "I have to." I choose to allow her to be herself. I choose to allow me to be me. I choose to shift.

Lynn: Yeah. But I choose to be there for my daughter. I couldn't imagine not being there at her last track meet and the big championship and she won it. So I was happy to sacrifice looking haggard to be there for her.

Aurora: And would you be willing to acknowledge and appreciate yourself for the amazing mom that you are and what you did by being there?

Lynn: Yes, yes.

Aurora: Great. You're a pretty amazing mom.

Lynn: Yeah. I feel blessed to have a daughter that I can do that for. I had an enjoyable day sitting in the sun. It was calming for me. And I had fun taking pictures of the kids.

Aurora: What does it tell you about your values and your priorities that you could appreciate?

Lynn: I really try to put my kids first. They lost their father and so I really try to be there for the times that are important to them, and I make sacrifices. You know, I could have been doing my own thing and relaxing, eating bonbons out on my deck on a beautiful sunny day. But I was happy that I was there to support her and to enjoy her victory and her happiness at her last track meet. So I was happy. And I was happy to be there at the prom when all the kids were getting dressed and see them having such fun and just being in the moment.

Aurora: And would you be willing to really acknowledge and appreciate who you are and how you show up in the world? Like hats off, kudos to you. I really admire and respect you for showing up even when you're very tired to walk in the truth of your values.

Lynn: Yeah. I feel blessed. I want to appreciate every moment that I have with my kids because you never know. With my husband or with my daughter, you never know if they'll be there tomorrow. So I'm glad I was doing that versus doing something else.

Aurora: Alright. Would you be willing to move on to the next step, Lynn?

Lynn: Yeah.

Aurora: Okay. So let's consider the contrary. We suffer when we don't see the whole truth and all the possibilities. So would you be willing to look at some other possibilities?

Lynn: Yeah.

Aurora: Now what's a contrary to "I need her to stop criticizing me"?

Lynn: "I need to stop criticizing myself"?

Aurora: Tell me how that's so.

Lynn: I need to stop accepting the criticism. I need to stop taking it personally. Not criticize myself. I did the best I could on that day and I was happy to be doing what I was doing, so I shouldn't criticize myself for what other people think of me.

Aurora: Yeah. Whatever people think of me is none of my business.

Lynn: None of my business. I love that quote.

Aurora: I love it too. Anything else you notice around "I need to stop criticizing myself"?

Lynn: I really struggle with the issue of putting my kids first. I'm always at the end of the day, the end of the list, but, you know, this won't go on forever. I probably do way too much. But I'm okay with it. I'm okay with my choices.

Aurora: So there's no need to criticize you when you're okay with your choices.

Lynn: Yeah, I'm okay.

Aurora: And you're in alignment. Your values are reflected in your actions.

Lynn: Right.

Aurora: That's good.

Lynn: And if I'm tired or I look haggard, so be it. That's not important to me.

Aurora: Yeah, I get that. I love that about you. So let's look at another contrary.

Lynn: I need to stop criticizing my mother.

Aurora: Okay. "I need to stop criticizing my mother." Could you tell me how that's so?

Aurora: Well, I think whatever mothers do for us it's out of love, it's out of caring and concern. So I need to stop criticizing her because I should realize that she really does love me and care about me. She's worrying about me getting sick.

Aurora: Right.

Lynn: It's interesting that her mother used to always say that to her, "you're going to get sick." She used to make her drink a raw egg and wine when she was nine years old. It was an old wives' tale.

Aurora: Let's bring you back to "I need to stop criticizing my mother." Is that true?

Lynn: Yes.

Aurora: Okay. Is it as true or truer than "I need her to stop criticizing me"?

Lynn: I need to stop criticizing her. That's a more peaceful place.

Aurora: Yes. That's more peaceful.

Lynn: I can have control over that. I can't have control over her, but I can have control over me not criticizing her.

Aurora: Yes, exactly. So it's good to observe what other people do and take responsibility for what you can change, which is your side.

Lynn: Yeah.

Aurora: So given this wisdom that you have discovered as you've looked at this issue of criticism, what do you consciously choose?

Lynn: To shift my attitude about criticism and just let it go.

Aurora: Nice. That sounds empowered and more peaceful.

Lynn: Mhmm.

Aurora: So how could this situation be calling forth your very best?

Lynn: Well, I think it's raising my consciousness level so that I don't get bogged down in what other people think of me. It's about being okay with who you are and the choices you make, and being at peace and not listening to those voices that come from other people.

Aurora: Nice. Would you be willing to make a declaration about not listening to other people's opinions?

Lynn: Yeah.

Aurora: What would it sound like?

Lynn: (enthusiastic declaration) I do solemnly swear to not take criticism personally!

Aurora: Nice. I love that.

Lynn: Whatever they think of me is none of my business.

Aurora: Exactly right! Anything else you'd like to share?

Lynn: No. I'm complete.

Aurora: How are you feeling now, Lynn?

Lynn: It's a total shift. The next time somebody criticizes me, I think it will be easier. The next time someone says something negative, I will remember this Peace Method® coaching. This is what I need to do. I love reminders like the words "shift happens" and "what other people think of me is none of my business."

This Peace Method® process allowed me to see all the angles. It really helps me to see it from everybody's perspective. And yet the only important one is my own perspective, and how I choose to live with my kids and help them based on them not having a father.

Aurora: Yes. And I acknowledge you for how you're showing up with such commitment.

Lynn: Thank you.

Aurora: And you're living in alignment with your values.

Lynn: (pleased) Because I could be sitting in my jammies watching TV eating bonbons and never get out of bed!

Aurora: Crisis: some people get better, some people get bitter, and some people get bonbons.

Lynn: Right. I love that one. Do you want to be bitter or do you want to get better? And it's definitely getting better.

Aurora: Absolutely.

Lynn: Thank you.

What I'd like to point out about this coaching is the value of listening. Once Lynn had the opportunity to vent her frustrations, she was very coachable and discovered her own deep wisdom. She realized that she was living in alignment with her authentic values.

"I'm going to fail"

Rose is a young widow whose husband committed suicide a year and a half ago. Rose has left her financially-rewarding but unfulfilling corporate career to help victims of domestic abuse. She's happy because she has just completed training with victim services.

But she's frustrated by her fear of failure. Her daughter has been expressing doubts, asking questions such as, "When are you going to get a real job?" and "What about all those years in university?" Rose's confidence is shaken by her daughter's doubts — and her own doubts. After Rose shares her fears, triumphs, and challenges, I coach her on a group training call at the Grief Coach Academy.

Aurora: So let's look at what's most sticky for you, so I can be of greater service. What's the thought that's most painful, the one that's a knife in your heart?

Rose: I worry that I'm going to fail. And I'm not doing enough. I need to do more, and I need to be more motivated.

Aurora: Alright. Well these are all good things to work on. Each one of these painful thoughts is draining your energy or motivation. So any one of these bricks would be good to look at using the Peace Method®. Listen with your whole heart and body and see which is most upsetting: "I'm not doing enough" … "I need to do more" … "I need to be more motivated" … "I'm going to fail."

Rose: I need to be more motivated.

Aurora: Is "I need to be more motivated" really more painful than "I'm going to fail"?

Rose: No.

Aurora: I didn't think so. "I'm going to fail" seems like it's the root of the issue, and "I need to be more motivated" is a strategy to deal with that painful thought. Can you hear that?

Rose: You're right.

Aurora: Yeah. So if you're willing, let's look at the root painful thought, "I'm going to fail." Does that work for you, honey?

Rose: Yeah.

Aurora: Okay. So everyone else, please do your own investigation around, "I'm going to fail" in whatever way failure might show up for you. It might be career. It might be relationship. It might be your new diet. It might be working out at the gym. It might be publishing your book. It might be a slightly different flavor, but I think "I'm going to fail" is a very common painful thought. It's part of the collective unconscious. So it's a wonderful one to investigate, explore, and release.

So let's take a couple of deep cleansing breaths, Rose. And come fully into the present moment. And then we'll do the Peace Method® on, "I'm going to fail."

Rose: Good.

Aurora: (brief meditation) So inhale and relax your body. Exhale and smile. Inhale coming fully into the present moment. And exhale knowing that it's a wonderful moment. And again with the deep breathing, relax, smile, present moment, wonderful moment. One more time, relax your body. Smile, remembering that this is a wonderful moment, and knowing that it's just a wonderful, precious moment.

(pause) So Rose, is this thought, "I'm going to fail," about the past, the present, or the future?

Rose: Present and future.

Aurora: Present?

Rose: I guess more the future.

Aurora: Maybe all the future, because "I'm going to" is the future.

Rose: Yes. Well I guess I feel a bit like I'm failing in the present, because I don't feel the motivation. So I have the fear of failing in the future.

Aurora: Alright, so "I'm failing." I've written that down. That's an adjacent brick to, "I'm going to fail." Very close, but distinct. So what I'm hearing from you is, "I'm going to fail," is a thought about the future. And what I know about the future is that we can never solve all potential future problems. And trying to do so is an insane recipe for stress. Does that make sense?

Rose: Yes.

Aurora: So tell me about what comes up for you when you think the thought, "I'm going to fail."

Rose: Financial stress. Disappointment. I think they're the two big ones.

Aurora: Okay. So when financial stress comes up, is that a cluster of other thoughts around financial worries?

Rose: Yes. But the thing is, I don't really have any reason to have that. But it's still there. But disappointment in myself and my family being disappointed in me, that is bigger than the financial.

Aurora: Alright. So take a deep breath, and just lean into this thought, "I'm going to fail." How does your body react?

Rose: It makes me tense, my neck, my back. It gives me a tense, uneasy feeling.

Aurora: And how do you treat yourself, with the thought, "I'm going to fail"?

Rose: When I should be writing in my book I don't.

Aurora: Uh-huh, so it doesn't actually help you?

Rose: It doesn't help me.

Aurora: It doesn't. It sabotages you.

Rose: I'm sabotaging myself, so I need to get past this. It's not something I have all the time. It's something I struggle with.

Aurora: So this thought "I'm going to fail" paralyzes or sabotages you, and does not help you.

Rose: Yes. It sabotages my day when I could be doing something, and then I'll do what I'm supposed to do, but I'll struggle my way through it like a robot.

Aurora: Right, instead of with joy. Any other thoughts, or feelings, or reactions that you would like to share that come up when you believe the thought, "I'm going to fail"?

Rose: Well, the disappointment thing because I'm writing a book, too. And it's such a sensitive subject that I'm writing about. I'm writing about suicide, and my story with the hope of helping other people. The fear of failure, it's not just for myself. I don't want to disappoint anyone.

Aurora: When your thought is around disappointing yourself, you're definitely in your own business. But when you have the thought, "I'm going to fail" and you're thinking about how other people will react, whose business are you in?

Rose: Well I can't control how other people act or react.

Aurora: Exactly right.

Rose: So I guess that's other people's business.

Aurora: Right. And when we're in other people's business, how do we feel?

Rose: Stressed?

Aurora: Stressed, exactly. I love that Wayne Dyer says to embrace, "What other people think of me is none of my business."

Rose: Good reminder.

Aurora: It's a great reminder. Notice with the thought, "I'm going to fail," stress, self-sabotage, tension, pain, and other painful thoughts come up. Doesn't help you write your book about suicide, so there's quite a cost associated with the thought, "I'm going to fail." Who would you be in this moment, <u>without</u> the thought, "I'm going to fail"?

Rose: I'd be further ahead. I could take on the world!

Aurora: Nice. Are you ready to move onto the next step, Rose?

Rose: Yeah.

Aurora: So with the thought, "I'm going to fail," would you be willing to just allow that thought to be there for a moment, and notice it, but without thinking, "Oh that's _my_ thought." But just, "Huh, there's that cloud up in the sky. It doesn't have anything to do with me. There's that thought, "I'm going to fail." I see you. I don't have to pick you up. Would it be possible for you to allow that thought in that way?

Rose: Yes.

Aurora: I love this great question I learned from Dr. Dain Heer. And the question is, "Who does this belong to?" So who does this thought, "I'm going to fail," belong to? Does it belong to you? Does it belong to people in your family? Or is it one of those sticky icky thoughts that's being broadcast from every city and every household? And that like some kind of beautiful, receptive, sensitive tuning fork—like a radio antennae—you're picking up the thought. Just like if you tuned the channel to the jazz station you would pick up jazz. Maybe you're hearing the thought, "I'm going to fail"—but maybe it's not yours. So who does it belong to?

Rose: Well that's true, because I'm not really saying it to myself. It's coming from around me. It's not that my family doesn't want me to succeed, because I know that they do, but they worry. They just worry because I'm doing this on my own, and I don't have that paycheck coming in every two weeks.

Aurora: Hmm, so when you notice that, and you're noticing that it's coming from them, what I'm hearing is there could be a possibility of a compassion for the worry and fear of your family, and kindness coming from you—as opposed to picking it up and letting it Velcro® to you as your identity.

Rose: Yeah. Well I'm not mad at them for it. I guess I'm frustrated with myself for allowing those thoughts to come into my head.

Aurora: Well, maybe that's part of what makes you a really great coach. Because you're a sensitive receiver like the antenna of a radio station.

Rose: Yeah.

Aurora: Yeah?

Rose: Yeah because nobody actually comes up and says it. I am a very sensitive receiver, and I take messages.

Aurora: Right. So just ask yourself "Who this does this belong to?" And if you notice, wow this doesn't even belong to me, you can just say, "Thanks for sharing," and —return to sender!

Rose: Yeah. I'd like to do that.

Aurora: Good. You'd like to do that. Would you be willing to do that right now?

Rose: Yes.

Aurora: Great. How does that feel?

Rose: That feels good.

Aurora: What can you appreciate around the thought, "I'm going to fail"?

Rose: That it's really not my thought.

Aurora: Yeah, good to appreciate.

Rose: Because I do truly believe that I can be successful.

Aurora: I know you can.

Rose: I truly believe that. I don't know why I let that come into my head and sabotage some of my days. I feel like punishing myself when that happens.

Aurora: And now you can make a different choice.

Rose: Yeah.

Aurora: So, wouldn't that be a wonderful thing to appreciate about this? That now you can give this gift to your coaching clients, a real discernment that thoughts are not personal? Like Byron Katie says, "Thoughts are like raindrops. Would you argue with a raindrop?" Does that resonate with you?

Rose: Yeah. I honestly don't take it personally. Because I know that the people I'm around are always looking out for my best interest. But they don't always know what that is.

Aurora: Well I'm hearing from you that it does sabotage your day when you pick it up.

Rose: Yes, it does.

Aurora: So this is a good awareness around not picking it up.

Rose: Yeah, where it actually affects my entire day, and sometimes it could affect my entire week.

Aurora: My experience is that the truth always makes us feel lighter and a lie will make us feel heavier. So if you're feeling heaviness, then it's not true. And the thought likely belongs to somebody else.

Rose: Mm-hmm.

Aurora: Are you ready to consider the contrary?

Rose: Sure.

Aurora: We suffer when we don't see the whole truth, and all the possibilities. So what is the contrary of, "I'm going to fail"?

Rose: I'm <u>not</u> going to fail.

Aurora: Tell me how that's true.

Rose: Because I'm going to recognize that feeling is just a cloud over my head, that I can send back.

Aurora: Nice. Tell me more about, "I'm not going to fail."

Rose: I'm not going to fail. I'm going to do the work that I need to do.

Aurora: Good.

Rose: Because to be successful, you need to do the work to get there.

Aurora: Exactly right. Tell me times that you've succeeded in the past.

Rose: (with conviction) Always.

Aurora: Always. You have 100% success ratio from the past?

Rose: Yes.

Aurora: That seems like pretty compelling evidence that "I'm not going to fail" is true!

Rose: I put my mind to something and I always succeed in the end. So I don't know why I would ever think that I would fail.

Aurora: Why would you?

Rose: I think the grief of dealing with my husband's suicide has taken a toll on my self-esteem. So I think that allows things to seep in, where normally in the past it wouldn't.

Aurora: That's real wisdom. It's normal and natural that grief — especially from a sudden and unexpected death — whacks our confidence and can erode our self-esteem. So I acknowledge that that's normal and natural, and very wise of you to notice that.

So, what we have learned from you is that "I'm <u>not</u> going to fail" is clearly true. You've always succeeded in the past — 100% of the time. When you put your mind to something, you succeed. You're not going to fail is true because you're going to do the work that you need to do. You're noticing that this thought, "I'm going to fail" doesn't even belong to you.

Rose: Yeah. It's a new feeling for me. It's not something I've suffered with my whole life.

Aurora: Yeah, so good to notice. And that's real wisdom, so you can make allowance for that, and be kind to you. So is, "I'm <u>not</u> going to fail" a true statement?

Rose: Yes.

Aurora: And is it as true or truer than, "I'm going to fail"?

Rose: It's truer that "I'm going to fail."

Aurora: Absolutely. Okay, so given all this wisdom that you have discovered by doing this simple process, what are you enthusiastic about, Rose?

Rose: Well I guess going through it, it just brought awareness where it's coming from. So I recognize that. And if it's the fear of others, then it's not my problem. It's their problem.

Aurora: Good.

Rose: And I do have the power to mail it away. Return to sender.

Aurora: Absolutely.

Rose: If I choose to.

Aurora: Yes.

Rose: And I <u>do</u> choose to.

Aurora: I celebrate that. Good work, honey. So how were you feeling at the beginning around this issue, "I'm going to fail" on a scale of 1 to 10, and how are you feeling now, with 1 being awful and 10 being top of the world?

Rose: I think probably at a 3 to start. And now I'm feeling pretty motivated, so I think I'm up around a 9. I think I'll go do some writing now.

Aurora: Great, so from 3 to a 9. That's wonderful! What would you like to share with the listeners, Rose, about doing the Peace Method®? What stood out to you?

Rose: When you asked, "Have I been successful in the past?" And my answer was yes, and then I thought, "Well why am I feeling this now?" I realized it is because of the grieving that I've gone through in the last year and a half. That is how it has affected me. So that was an important insight. It's not really who I am.

Aurora: Nice. That's a great deal of wisdom, and I love that you can notice where it's actually coming from. And you can kindly, gently, and sweetly make an allowance for that, while not picking it up as who you are. But you can none-the-less make an allowance for that, and be kind to yourself. Give yourself a hug and then get back to writing. Thank you for sharing.

Rose: It was a very helpful exercise for me, and I'm glad that I had the opportunity to work through it.

Aurora: I'm glad. "I'm going to fail" is a universal painful thought. I believe that it doesn't belong to you. That it's part of the collective unconscious that you're simply receiving. Like mail.

Rose: (laughs) Return to sender!

Aurora: Exactly, return to sender.

Rose: I like that one. I'm going to remember that. Thank you.

Aurora: You're welcome.

In this example, Rose discovered some unexpected side effects of her grief. Her husband's suicide a year and a half ago undermined her confidence and self-esteem. She reclaimed her confidence and went from 3 to a 9 out of 10 in about fifteen minutes of coaching.

"He's not working on himself"

Donna is kind, spiritual, and insightful. She is a student at the Grief Coach Academy. Donna is emotionally raw on the heels of breaking up with her boyfriend, and moving out of their shared home. Donna has been working on self-improvement for years, so she has a number of tools in her toolbox.

No matter how many tools and processes people learn, it is normal and natural to feel grief when an important relationship ends or changes form, as some hopes and dreams for the future die. After discussing a number of painful thoughts, Donna realized that "he is not working on himself" was her most painful thought about her ex-boyfriend. That's where we join this coaching demonstration, which was part of a group training call at the Grief Coach Academy.

Aurora: So let's all support Donna by taking some deep cleansing breaths. Donna can lead the charge as we look at the painful thought "He is not working on himself." Do you have that thought about someone in your life?

(meditation inspired by Thich Nhat Hanh) Inhale and relax your body. Exhale and smile; inhale coming fully into the present moment, and exhale knowing that it's a wonderful moment and again, breathing at your own pace. Inhale and relax. Exhale and smile; inhale coming fully into the present moment and exhale knowing that it's a wonderful moment.

So Donna, "he is not working on himself" — is that a thought about the past, the present or the future?

Donna: Somewhere between the present and the future. I think it's more future.

Aurora: Okay.

Donna: Yes, it is more future.

Aurora: More future, good to notice. You can never solve all potential future problems. The present is your place of power.

So how do you react when you believe the thought "he is not working on himself"? What happens?

Donna: I get upset and frustrated. I have sadness come up, like deep sadness and some anger. I have concern that — I know that at the depth of it there is a selfish concern that he'll never be available in a way that I would like him to be. Yeah.

Aurora: So that's another painful thought: "He'll never be available in the way I'd like him to be." It would be good to look at that thought separately. But just coming back to the thought "he's not working on himself" when and where did that thought first occur to you?

Donna: Months ago, months and months ago when it all started unraveling.

Aurora: So whose business are you in when you think the thought he's not working on himself?

Donna: I know this one. I'm clearly in Peter's business.

Aurora: Yes.

Donna: Clearly, and it's hard to stay out of it.

Aurora: When we are in other people's business we always feel lonely and stressed and separated and disempowered—always, always, always. Does this thought "he's not working on himself" bring peace or stress into your life?

Donna: It's stressful.

Aurora: I'm not asking you to drop the thought, but just imagine for a moment that it's no longer possible for you to believe the thought "he's not working on himself." How would you be?

Donna: I wouldn't be so worried. I wouldn't be so stuck thinking things aren't going to get better. I would be more concerned with my world, what I need to work on.

Aurora: Good. Any other thoughts or feelings you'd like to express before we move on to the A of the Peace Method®?

Donna: Yeah. There is just the pain of me needing him to get this. It's really so disempowering. I can really swim in that, and I know it doesn't serve me.

Aurora: So that's another painful thought. You might write down, "I need him to get this" and do the Peace Method® on that thought. Thank you for sharing. Are you ready to move on?

Donna: Yes, I am.

Aurora: So, as you know, the A of the Peace Method® is around acceptance and/or appreciation. I'm going to invite you to look at this thought, "he's not working on himself." Maybe that's just what is so. Maybe that is a neutral observation. Would you be willing to make space for that, to allow that, in this moment, "he is not working on himself" without fighting against it, resisting it, or making it wrong?

Donna: Yeah.

Aurora: Good.

Donna: If I just accept that that is what's happening, yeah, it puts me in a place of not arguing with reality.

Aurora: Yes.

Donna: Yeah, I can find acceptance for that.

Aurora: Much more peaceful when you just allow "he's not working on himself" in the same way that you might look out the window and go "oh, it's raining, I better bring my umbrella." It's not personal and it doesn't say anything about what it might be doing two hours from now or tomorrow or the next week.

Donna: Yeah.

Aurora: So can you allow and accept "he's not working on himself" with that same energy? Like oh, it's raining?

Donna: Yeah, there is a little disappointment, but I don't have to take it personally. It didn't rain today just to ruin my life.

Aurora: Right, exactly right. And just like it didn't rain today to ruin your life the rain is bringing something of value. It keeps the plants green. So in the same way is there something you could possibly appreciate about "he's not working on himself"?

Donna: Well, is he really the partner that I want?

Aurora: Correct me if I'm wrong, but what I'm hearing is that you could appreciate that if he is somebody who doesn't work on himself ever, that that's a clue that he's not the right partner for you. Is that what you're saying?

Donna: Yes, exactly.

Aurora: Okay. What else could you appreciate about the thought "he's not working on himself" or about the situation?

Donna: Maybe he doesn't need to work on himself. Maybe he's really happy with where he's at. A part of me doesn't believe that, but who am I to say really?

Aurora: Right.

Donna: That's him not stepping out of his comfort zone. That might be very comfortable. And what else is there to appreciate about "he's not working on himself"? It brings me back to me. I can only work on myself. I can only do my own work and that's the reminder.

Aurora: So how could that reminder serve you in a beneficial way?

Donna: Because I'd stop looking over there. I'd stop looking out the window and saying oh it's raining and I'd look at what else is happening that I can actually do.

Aurora: That sounds wise.

Donna: Yeah.

Aurora: Would you be willing to move on to consider the contrary now or is there anything else you want to share about acceptance or appreciation?

Donna: No, that feels good.

Aurora: In my experience, we suffer when we don't see all the possibilities. So what is another possibility looking at an opposite or contrary statement to "he is not working on himself"?

Donna: Well there are two that I see right off. One is "I'm not working on myself."

Aurora: Tell me about that.

Donna: Well mostly I am working on myself and I'd like to take some credit for that. But there are ways that I get really caught up in "Peter is not doing his work" and so I can't be doing my work when I'm doing that.

Aurora: Right, exactly.

Donna: They can't be happening simultaneously.

Aurora: Right.

Donna: And it brings me stress when I do that. It brings me sadness. I get stuck in some old place that is no longer appropriate.

Aurora: Okay, so what I'm hearing from you is "I'm not working on myself" is true, especially when you're looking at Peter.

Donna: Right.

Aurora: What's the other contrary that came up for you?

Donna: He is working on himself.

Aurora: Tell me how that is so.

Donna: It just doesn't look how I think it should.

Aurora: Okay.

Donna: I think that he has made amazing progress in being transparent, which is a big issue. He has made amazing progress in being able to talk about what's happening for him. He is really a guy. He is a man's man and so what "him working on himself" and what "me working on myself" look like are really different.

Aurora: Good wisdom. That sounds pretty enlightened to me!

Donna: Yeah. Also the fact that we've made this separation and have still managed to stay really close—he has to have been working on himself in order to do that.

Aurora: Exactly right. It takes two to do that.

Donna: Yeah, it does.

Aurora: That's pretty extraordinary.

Donna: Yeah, it has been really extraordinary.

Aurora: It takes quite an evolved man to be able to do that.

Donna: Yeah.

Aurora: So what we're learning from you is that "he is working on himself" is true. It just doesn't look like you thought it would, but he's really made progress in transparency. He's a man's man, so it's going to look different than it will look for you. He is working on himself is true as evidenced by the fact that you're still close in spite of the separation. So given that evidence, would you say "he is working on himself" is a true statement?

Donna: Yeah, I would say that, yes.

Aurora: Is it as true or truer than "he's not working on himself"?

Donna: It's just as true.

Aurora: As true, good. Do you want to look at another contrary to "he is not working on himself"?

Donna: He is not working on himself. He is working on himself. I am not working on myself.

Aurora: Well I don't want to leave you with just looking at "I'm not working on myself" so why don't we flip that one more time to acknowledge that "I am working on myself"? Can you tell me how it's true that you are working on yourself?

Donna: Well I'm here with you.

Aurora: There you go. That's evidence.

Donna: I was brave enough to speak up again.

Aurora: Yes, that takes courage.

Donna: Yeah, I've been brave enough to hold the space for love. I think that I've been—yeah, there are so many ways that I've been working on myself. I'm studying at the Grief Coach Academy. That's working on myself.

Aurora: Yes, absolutely. So "I am working on myself"—true statement. Yes?

Donna: Yes.

Aurora: Great. Okay, so given all this wisdom that you have discovered what are you enthusiastic about now?

Donna: What am I enthusiastic about? I'm in this place of absolute freedom. I'm not attached to a job or a place to live or a man. I'm not in partnership. I have two lovely children and they're taken care of for a month or two and I have an incredible amount of freedom right now. The flipside to that is it can be like loss or fear or it can be enthusiasm and freedom. There is my choice. I'd rather have enthusiasm about my freedom.

Aurora: I agree. What do you consciously choose around your relationship with Peter?

Donna: Just loving what is; yeah, just loving where we're at.

Aurora: Good wisdom, really lovely, Donna. Are you complete or is there anything else you want to share?

Donna: The whole process that Peter and I been going through has run parallel to my joining the Grief Coach Academy, so I feel so supported going through this. All the tools that we use, I use them in my life all the time. I am just so grateful for this happening simultaneously.

Aurora: Well you are loved and supported, and I'm glad that it has been helpful. That's wonderful. Thank you for sharing, Donna. Are you complete?

Donna: Yeah, I am.

Aurora: Good work. That was some heavy lifting there, an important issue that is really fresh. How do you feel now after doing the Peace Method®, which took maybe all of 15 minutes. It was really quick.

Donna: That thought that we were just working on has been really heavy. The reminder that I'm not in my own business was important. I would say I've gone from maybe a 3 to a 6.5 on a scale of 1 to 10.

Aurora: Excellent progress!

Donna: Yeah, absolutely.

Aurora: You said that the thought felt heavy. What if the truth always makes us feel lighter? So when we're feeling heavy that's a good clue that it's not true. Use the Peace Method® or another one of the processes we teach at the Grief Coach Academy to discover the truth. Anything else you'd like to share?

Donna: I think that even in some really unconventional places — the places where people want to assign blame and it's very clearly somebody's else's fault, there is betrayal or whatever — that you can find peace and love even in those places and the Peace Method® is a really beautiful tool for that. I love it for that.

Aurora: I love it too. And you are a beautiful demonstration, a living, breathing, walking example of how you can find love and compassion and connection even in a difficult situation like a breakup. Kudos to you, Donna.

One thing I'd like to point out from this coaching session is that after Donna discovered some truth in "I am not working on myself"—which gave her valuable insight, I didn't leave it there. As "I am not working on myself" could leave her with a heavy feeling, I invited her to consider the contrary of that, and look at "I am working on myself" which felt much lighter and was true.

Donna did some deep work on a painful thought, and made amazing progress with only fifteen minutes of coaching. As a coach, don't try to be a "fast food" coach. Faster isn't better. Take your time, be patient, and celebrate progress. Even a slight shift in awareness or peace of mind is precious. It plants seeds that will blossom in due time, especially if you continue to water your client's growing happiness with ongoing coaching.

"I need her to share"

Victor is a thoughtful, mature man whose wife died of breast cancer twenty years ago. He is a student at the Grief Coach Academy. He is getting back on the dating scene and is frustrated with the woman he's seeing.

Victor: I am frustrated at Julia because she doesn't speak and share her feelings or experiences. She should express her feelings more so I can understand her more.

Aurora: And who is Julia to you?

Victor: Just someone I recently met, and we've struck up somewhat of a relationship at this time, but she is a little reticent about expressing her feelings and experiences with me. She should verbalize more.

Aurora: Well she couldn't be with anybody better to help her open up to that, Victor. Would you like to play?

Victor: Sure, I'd enjoy playing.

Aurora: Excellent. So let's see which thought you'd like to do the Peace Method® on. What do you think is the stickiest, ickiest, most painful thought around this issue with Julia?

Victor: The hardest part is, it's hard for me to understand where she's coming from, what her feelings are. I think the frustrating part is I seem to carry the conversation and she doesn't say a whole bunch, especially about her own experiences, so it almost becomes a one-way situation, more like 80/20. I do 80% of the talking and she does 20%. I'd like to have a bit more balance. That way I can also understand where she's coming from and I can offer my support, or whatever is needed at the time.

Aurora: It sounds like "I need her to share" is the painful thought?

Victor: Yes.

Aurora: Okay. Would you be willing to do the Peace Method® on "I need her to share"?

Victor: Yes.

Aurora: Okay. So let's just begin with a little breathing meditation. I'll lead us in it, but breathe at your own pace.

(deep breathing meditation) Inhale and relax your body. Exhale and smile. Inhale coming fully into the present moment, and exhale knowing that it's a wonderful moment. And again, inhale and relax. Exhale and smile. Inhale coming fully into the present moment, and exhale knowing that it's a wonderful moment.

So Victor, I'm curious. Is the thought "I need her to share" about the past, the present or the future?

Victor: Probably more the present, maybe some of her past. Yeah, what's happening now.

Aurora: All right, so mostly the present, and that is your point of power. Of course we cannot change the past, but we can choose and act in the present. So how do you feel when you believe the thought "I need her to share" and you're carrying 80% of the conversation?

Victor: It's frustrating, yeah, frustration.

Aurora: How do you treat Julia with the thought "I need her to share" and she's not sharing very much?

Victor: I feel like I'm carrying the burden of the conversation. When I have to do that, I'm not going to be able to learn about someone else. The listening part is the important part. That's why we have two ears and one mouth. It's like how do I get to know you and understand you and where you're coming from? It's a bit frustrating and I'm wondering, is there something that you're hiding?

Aurora: So how do you react in that situation where you're carrying 80% of the conversation? Do you ask her questions like how do I get to know you and understand you? Do you redouble your efforts to carry the conversation or do you do the opposite? What shows up?

Victor: I start to talk maybe a little bit more or I may ask her some questions. Usually even when she does answer, it's not a real long elaboration. It's like pulling teeth.

Aurora: So I'm curious. Whose business are you in with the thought "I need her to share"?

Victor: I would say it sounds like it's her business.

Aurora: What you need in a relationship is your business in my experience. But who she is, is her business. Does that resonate with you, or does it feel like it's all her business to you?

Victor: I don't think it's all her business because in a relationship there is a give and take, and the scales aren't balanced out properly.

Aurora: Right.

Victor: So a little bit more balance in those scales.

Aurora: A little more balance. Do you feel like you've expressed your thoughts and feelings enough? Would you be willing to go to the next step or is there something else you'd like to share?

Victor: Yeah, pretty much. We could go to the next step.

Aurora: All right. So with the thought "I need her to share" would you be willing to just allow her to be who she is, which apparently seems to be somebody who sometimes doesn't share, or perhaps it's at this stage of a relationship that she's not so loquacious? Would you be willing to just allow that without making a war on it?

Victor: Yeah, I can allow that.

Aurora: Good. Does that feel lighter?

Victor: Yeah. I definitely don't want to make war.

Aurora: That's not your brand. What could you possibly appreciate either about the thought "I need her to share" or about the situation?

Victor: I've only known her since February, so we don't know each other very well and I understand that she's had some bad experiences. She had a bad marriage, so maybe she is a little reticent in expressing her feelings. So I can be patient. I'm just recoiling from saying that P word "patience."

Aurora: It's a dirty word! (laughs) I know that's one of my lessons this lifetime, to have more patience. God is giving me ample opportunity to learn this lesson. Is that how you feel?

Victor: Actually just saying that really made it a lot lighter. I'm realizing it's okay to give her some space and just see what happens.

Aurora: How could this be an opportunity to change a pattern in relationships that hasn't been serving you up until now?

Victor: Be more understanding and more patient, Go more with the flow.

Aurora: Nice, that sounds light.

Victor: Mm-hmm.

Aurora: Are you complete on that step?

Victor: Yeah.

Aurora: Are you willing to consider the contrary?

Victor: Sure.

Aurora: Okay. In my experience, we suffer when we don't see the whole truth and all the possibilities. So what are some other possibilities that we could explore together? What is the contrary of "I need her to share"?

Victor: I come up with "I need to be." I look at it now and see I wasn't being me as much as I thought.

Aurora: Tell me more about "I need to be."

Victor: I need to be in my power.

Aurora: Nice.

Victor: I've been giving away my power too much in this. Some old baggage came up there I guess.

Aurora: Good to notice.

Victor: Yeah, I didn't realize it. I couldn't see the forest for the trees.

Aurora: How else is it true "I need to be"?

Victor: When I am being me, this is me. I need to be myself and relax and be more in the moment.

Aurora: Nice wisdom, sounds like enlightenment to me.

Victor: Yeah.

Aurora: Would you be willing to look at another contrary to "I need her to share" just changing, adding or subtracting one word?
(pause) Do you need some help?

Victor: Sure. I'm having trouble formulating some words.

Aurora: Some possibilities, keeping it simple, would be: "I don't need her to share" or "I need me to share" or it might be "she needs me to share" or it might be "she needs to share." Any one of those seem interesting to investigate?

Victor: "She needs to share."

Aurora: Well let's look at that one then. So she needs to share, like she needs herself to share. Would you like to investigate it from that point of view? The painful thought was "I need her to share," so if we looked at "she needs her to share" it's not proper English, but it captures what we're going for.

Victor: Yeah, that's better.

Aurora: Okay. So "she needs her to share" — tell me how that's so, that she needs herself to share. It's awkward English, but it helps us focus on the contrary. So tell me about "she needs herself to share."

Victor: Well when she does share, it's really good and we can talk for hours. I can be me.

Aurora: And you need to be you, so that works out nicely.

Victor: That's right.

Aurora: Yeah. Anything else you notice around how it's true that "she needs her to share"?

Victor: We laugh more, so that's always good.

Aurora: Agreed. What is your experience with women in general? Do they need to share? Is that something that usually works for women (or people) that when they share it meets a need they have themselves?

Victor: Yes and that's one of the things I attempt to elicit — allowing people to share their feelings and experiences.

Aurora: Well hasn't she done a beautiful job of attracting the perfect man to help her share?

Victor: Thank you.

Aurora: You're welcome, Victor. So let's just consider the initial painful thought was "I need her to share" and then we looked at "I need to be." Which one is more true: "I need to be" or "I need her to share"?

Victor: I need to be, be me.

Aurora: Yes, more true. Forgive the awkward English, but we looked at "she needs her to share" versus "I need her to share." Which one is more true?

Victor: Say those two again.

Aurora: "I need her to share" was your initial painful thought, and then we looked at "she needs her to share." We discovered the truth that when she has shared, she's more relaxed, the conversation flows, you can go on talking for hours. When she does, you can be you. You both laugh more. And that "she needs her to share" is also true because you notice with people in general it's very helpful when they share. So which is more true, "she needs her to share" or "I need her to share"?

Victor: She needs her to share.

Aurora: Okay. Good to notice. Are you ready to move onto the next step?

Victor: Yes.

Aurora: Wonderful. So given all this wisdom that you have discovered today Victor, what are you enthusiastic about now?

Victor: I feel clear about the situation now.

Aurora: Nice.

Victor: More clarity and more insight and I realized that a bit of old baggage from old relationships came out there.

Aurora: Good to notice.

Victor: Yeah, I can realize now that's okay, that's the past and but I'm now in the present. And that now is what I'm going to focus on.

Aurora: Nice. And how does this inform your choice of how you're going to be the next time you're with Julia?

Victor: I'm just going to be me.

Aurora: I celebrate that! Wonderful. Are you complete, Victor?

Victor: Yes, thank you very much.

Aurora: You're so welcome. So how did you feel on a scale of one to ten at the beginning, and how do you feel now?

Victor: I probably started out around maybe a three, and now I'd say I'm at nine.

Aurora: Nice, that's a big shift. What would you like to share with your fellow Grief Coach Academy students around your experience doing the Peace Method®?

Victor: It's fabulous! I'm looking forward to reaching out to those people who need my services in using the Peace Method® too. Especially the men, if I can do this here myself and see the results I know that it's going to help a lot of men out there when they move through their losses.

Aurora: Absolutely. You can do this. It's going to make a big difference to all the people you serve, all your coaching clients—and to Julia, too!

As a coach, trust your intuition, and take your time so your client can discover their own wisdom and insight. Although Victor's contrary "I need to be me" was not a direct opposite to "I need her to share" there was a conviction in his voice, so I sensed that it would be valuable for him to explore. The ideal attitude of a coach is neutral curiosity. Victor gained a lot of insight and wisdom very quickly with this simple process.

"The nanny needs to be able to say "no" to Belle"

Elizabeth is a busy mother with several young children and a demanding job. She wants her nanny to enforce the house rules with Elizabeth's three-year-old daughter.

Elizabeth: I am angry at Maryanne—she's my nanny—for letting Belle eat on the couch. She should realize that Belle makes a mess. And she should understand that the furniture is expensive and try and take care of it. I need Maryanne to pay better attention to the things she's letting Belle do. But I love Maryanne. She's dependable, reliable, she's pleasant, she's happy; she's everything you could ever want in a caregiver. But Maryanne needs to be able to say no to Belle.

Aurora: Thank you for sharing. Would you like to do the Peace Method® on "Maryanne needs to be able to say no to Belle"?

Elizabeth: Yes, absolutely.

Aurora: So, Elizabeth, let's take a couple of deep, cleansing breaths and come fully into the present moment.

(meditation) So inhale and relax your body. Exhale and smile. Inhale coming fully into the present moment. And exhale knowing that it's a wonderful moment.

So with this thought, "Maryanne needs to be able to say no to Belle"—is that the thought you'd like to work, is that the most sticky icky one that comes up for you?

Elizabeth: Yes.

Aurora: Okay. So I'm curious. Is this thought "Maryanne needs to be able to say no to Belle" about the past, the present, or the future?

Elizabeth: All three.

Aurora: Good to notice. We can never change the past and we can never solve all potential future problems, but we can deal with the right here and right now. So tell me, what comes up for you when you believe the thought "Maryanne needs to be able to say no to Belle"?

Elizabeth: Belle is very strong-willed and she needs structure, and when things are loosey-goosey then she gets off track. So it's important that there's structure and sometimes you have to say no to a three-year-old.

Aurora: So how do you treat Maryanne with the thought "Maryanne needs to be able to say no to Belle"?

Elizabeth: I try to remind her that she's the grownup, I try to say that often—you're the adult, she's the child, just say no.

Aurora: Right. And how do you treat Belle with the thought "Maryanne needs to be able to say no to Belle"?

Elizabeth: I probably get frustrated at Belle because she knows the rules and I say, just because Maryanne doesn't tell you to sit at the table, sit at the table, like that. So maybe I'm not the nicest.

Aurora: Are there any other thoughts or feelings that happen when you believe the thought "Maryanne needs to be able to say no to Belle"?

Elizabeth: No. Just frustrated. I get frustrated at how there's too much spoiling.

Aurora: And did this thought first occur to you with that incident you shared about eating on the couch, or is this an ongoing thing?

Elizabeth: Oh good Lord, no. It's been going on—it's been going on since we adopted her. It's been going on for years with all the kids.

Aurora: Right. Are you feeling fully expressed? Ready for the next step?

Elizabeth: Yeah.

Aurora: Okay. So every cloud has a silver lining if you're willing to look for it. Are you willing?

Elizabeth: Absolutely.

Aurora: Okay. So I'm just wondering if you would be willing to allow the possibility that Maryanne, apparently, is not able to say no to Belle. Would you be willing to just allow that in your universe without having to make a war on it and just notice oh well, that's interesting, that's not one of Maryanne's strong points.

Elizabeth: Yes, I can do that.

Aurora: Good. What could there possibly be to appreciate about this situation with Maryanne and Belle?

Elizabeth: Well, I think that's obvious. She just loves her to death and she cares about her so much. She's so soft-hearted that she hates to see the kids upset.

Aurora: Nice.

Elizabeth: So I can appreciate her—I <u>do</u> appreciate her. I appreciate everything about her. It's just this one thing.

Aurora: Right.

Elizabeth: But I wouldn't want her to be a tyrant either. So it's a very difficult balancing act when you're not the parent. And I fully understand that so I appreciate that she's trying.

Aurora: So how could this be an opportunity to change a pattern that doesn't serve you?

Elizabeth: Well, I could let it go. I could stop trying to change it. I mean she's been with us for six years and it hasn't changed in six years.

Aurora: That sounds more peaceful. So let's move on to considering the contrary. We suffer when we don't see the whole truth and all the possibilities. Would you be willing to consider some other possibilities?

Elizabeth: Yes.

Aurora: Okay. Looking at "Maryanne needs to be able to say no to Belle." What would be a contrary of that, just changing, adding or subtracting one word?

Elizabeth: Maryanne needs to be able to say yes to Belle.

Aurora: I like that.

Elizabeth: You know what? So do I after I say it. She does need to be able to say yes to her.

Aurora: Okay. Tell me more about that.

Elizabeth: It's always so much better to be positive to children than negative. Sometimes she needs to be able to say yes. I would not want her saying no all the time. So yes, she does need to be able to say yes to her.

Aurora: What I'm hearing in your voice is that "Maryanne needs to be able to say yes to Belle" is true, yes?

Elizabeth: Yeah, it's true, absolutely.

Aurora: Is it as true, or perhaps truer than "Maryanne needs to be able to say no to Belle"?

Elizabeth: As true, absolutely. I think there's a balance, so I'm not sure if it's more true — maybe it's more true, but there still needs to be a balance.

Aurora: Good. Do you want to look at "I need to be able to say yes to Belle"?

Elizabeth: Yes, I need to be able to say yes to Belle.

Aurora: Okay. Tell me about that.

Elizabeth: Well, as a parent we say no, no, no, no, no all the time, especially to a two and three-year-old. And maybe I need to say yes more often. And that would definitely be more true.

Aurora: Nice. How does that feel when you notice that "I need to be able to say yes to Belle" is more true?

Elizabeth: It feels good. I think I know that, but it's hard, right? It's more natural to stop them from doing things than to allow them to do things.

Aurora: Yes. But you're very wise to say that it's important to be more positive to children than negative and all those nos take their toll.

Elizabeth: Yeah.

Aurora: Alright. So what we've learned is that "I need to be able to say yes to Belle" is more true than "Maryanne needs to be able to say no to Belle." That's good. So given all this wisdom that you've discovered by looking at this step-by-step, what are you enthusiastic about doing or being now, Elizabeth?

Elizabeth: I'm going to really try to let some of that control go, and try to be more flexible and not quite so rigid with the kids, and try to just relax a bit more and let them do a little more.

Aurora: That sounds peaceful.

Elizabeth: Yeah. Say yes to them a little more often.

Aurora: Right. What was this process like for you?

Elizabeth: It was good because this is something that's been bothering me for a while. It's not going to bother me as much now. It was good to work through it. It was very good to go through that and see things differently. When I first wrote it down I thought there's no way I could come out of the other side seeing it differently, but I have. So that's fantastic. Thank you.

Aurora: You're welcome.

"It's a terrible thing that my son got fired"

My 26-year-old son called me yesterday to say that he got fired after just 6 weeks at a new job earning $60,000 per year. I thought his life and career were launched with this dream job in his field, his second job in his field since he graduated with his Bachelor's degree.

I feel upset and worried. I call a friend and talk about it, I feel heard and loved but still feel angst and turmoil. I go for a walk and do the Peace Method® —which provided insight, clarity, and greater peace of mind. Here's what it sounded like:

"It's a terrible thing that my son got fired."

P = Present

This is partly about the present, but the catastrophizing comes from projecting into the future with fear and anxiety. I can't know the future. I can't solve all potential future problems.

E = Express

I feel like a bad Mom, like I failed to teach him well, failed to give him a proper work ethic, failed to tell him to show up with the intention of being worth 10x what they are paying him. I feel shame. I feel a heaviness. I feel alone—who can I share this with? I don't want to feel worse, and I don't want to share with people my son wouldn't want me to tell (although everyone will know soon enough).

I feel curious that I intuitively felt he was going to get fired, then I feel upset with myself that I didn't call Yale or do something useful in response to that intuition. I feel worried that we will be back in the same old co-dependent dance. I feel worried that he will ask to live with me and never move out. I feel worried that he will never get his act together. I feel worried that he is self-sabotaging. I blame myself. I feel like crap. (I realize now that these are mostly thoughts, not feelings.)

I know this situation belongs to Yale. It is his business if he has a job or not. But I feel "hooked" on failing him as a Mom. And I feel this problem may land in my lap, and become my business, if he returns home or wants to work for me again.

A = Accept / Appreciate

Acceptance? Yes, what is, is.

What can I appreciate? I can appreciate that my son and I have a close, loving, communicative relationship. That he calls me and tells me the truth. He shares his doubts and fears. I can appreciate that this could be his "wake up call" and a turning point—if he decides things must change. In my experience, the worst things can often turn out to be the best things.

I can appreciate that he's in no danger. He's healthy, he has an apartment, he has a car, he has food, they gave him a small severance, so he has a little bit of time to figure out what to do.

I can appreciate that he is the person who needs to figure out what to do—not me. It's his life, not mine.

I can appreciate that setbacks are part of life. How we respond to them separates "the men from the boys" as my late husband would say.

I can appreciate that he did manage to get a great job paying him $60,000 per year in his industry. He can get another one.

I can appreciate that he's in San Francisco, and that's a great place to get a new job.

I can appreciate that I supported him to move to San Francisco and gave him $5,000—and so I feel "done" on the support. I have been generous. His life is up to him now. He's 26—he's a man.

C = Consider the Contrary

On my walk, I considered a few contraries to my painful thought "It's a terrible thing that my son got fired."

"It's <u>not</u> a terrible thing that my son got fired."

Well, it's not terrible. Two months ago he didn't have this great job. Now he doesn't have it again. So he's back to square one. It's not really like he's in the hole. And he has had a valuable life experience that may change his life.

It's not terrible. It's not like he found out he has cancer. He didn't have a car accident and hurt himself or someone else. He didn't get a girl pregnant. He's not in jail after destroying someone's property like another friend's son. He doesn't have brain damage. He's not in a wheelchair unable to work. So it's not terrible.

He's smart, he's healthy. He's ambitious and hard-working when he wants to be. The truth is, it is <u>not</u> terrible.

It's a good thing that my son got fired.

He had a taste of success, a taste of making good money, having respect, having his life together. He could decide — no matter what, I am going to succeed! This challenge may inspire him to greatness.

I don't know why he got fired — but he does. He's very bright. This is a wake-up call to inspire him to be his very best.

I feel much more peaceful now.

E = Enthusiasm

I am enthusiastic about <u>not</u> protecting or coddling my son from his feelings — or from the situation. I feel enthusiastic about <u>not</u> emasculating him by solving his problems or telling him what to do.

I feel enthusiastic about expressing confidence in his ability to solve his own problems. He's smart and strategic, capable and competent, he can come up with a creative solution. I'm enthusiastic about remaining clear that I don't want him (or us) to go backwards. I want him to move forward and create his life his way.

I'm enthusiastic about finishing this book and including a number of real-life examples, like this one. I'm enthusiastic that doing the Peace Method® helped me a <u>lot</u>. Walking through the five steps really works to bring peace and clarity.

"My son will never get his act together"

I continue to explore other painful thoughts that are in the same cluster around this issue of my son getting fired. The next painful thought is:

"My son will never get his act together."

P = Present

I am in the future, projecting future outcomes. Good to notice. Still on my walk, I take some deep breaths and come back into the here and now.

E = Express

I feel contracted. I feel the opposite of freedom. Tight. Fear. Shame. I think I am a failure as a Mom, I failed to teach him properly. I feel ashamed of my son.

A = Acceptance

"My son will never get his act together." As I allow that possibility I feel a major shift to a softness and acceptance. Non-resistance. Stress evaporates.

That might be true. And then what? I would still love and cherish and appreciate my son. I would love him anyway—while loving myself and protecting my own happiness, life, boundaries, and financial well-being. There is a sweetness as I realize that I love my son whether he gets his act together or not. I love him no matter what.

C = Contrary

"My son <u>will</u> get his act together."
He is improving. Actually, he has grown enormously in the last few years. He is growing up. He has his act together in many ways: he's a good friend, he's smart, he got his degree, he's a good game designer, a good son, we have a close, open, communicative

relationship. He's respectful and pleasant to be around. He's presentable, he's good with his grandparents. Losing this job is an experience that will give him wisdom.

"I will never get my act together" (as a Mom)

Some truth there. I have some blind spots. I choose to be patient with myself.

"I will get my act together" (as a Mom)

I am determined that I <u>will</u> get my act together as a Mom! I'm learning and growing. I learned Non-violent Communication with Marshall Rosenburg, and that gave me much better ways to communicate my needs to my son, and talk to him about his needs without making either of us wrong.

I studied under Allison Armstrong and learned how to understand men better, and learned some ways that I was unintentionally emasculating Yale. Now I am much better about not solving his problems for him, or telling him what to do, or micro-managing him, or protecting him from his feelings (all of which are emasculating). Instead, I remind him of his strengths and express confidence in his ability to solve his problems. That's much more powerful, and leaves him as a man.

So the truth is, I <u>am</u> getting my act together as a Mom. I choose to be patient and kind with myself.

"My son <u>will</u> get his act together."

Whenever he decides to make something happen, it does happen. He applied for one scholarship and got a $60,000 scholarship. He didn't even apply for any jobs and got offered a $60,000/year job. They found him.

He wanted a new car and got one all by himself on the strength of the new job. He decided to learn Unity and many other programs, and he did. If he decides to find a new job or finish his game, he will! Yesterday when we spoke he seemed determined to get his act together, clear about what he wants, and clear about what went wrong, and what he can do better from now on. That sounds like someone in the process of getting his life together.

E = Enthusiasm

I'm enthusiastic about giving him some time and space to figure it out. I'm enthusiastic about continuing to empower rather than emasculate him. I'm enthusiastic about helping him not just feel better—but <u>be</u> better. I'm enthusiastic about keeping in touch to provide loving support. I'm enthusiastic that his apartment is paid for until the end of the month, and he got $1,500 in severance, so that provides a little time for him to solve his own problems.

This simple process helped me discover patience and wisdom. It's now three months later, I am witnessing my son "getting his act together." He has been working out at the gym every day. He listened to the Anthony Robbins CDs I gave him. He's turned away from fast foods in favor of eating healthy foods.

He's grown wiser and is becoming a man. He's been working on his own video game, and is in the process of raising money on www.Kickstarter.com so that he can get funding to complete it. Whether he succeeds at raising the money or not, he is following his passion and is driven to create the life of his dreams.

To acknowledge this, I wrote him this note on August 18, 2012:

> *Dear Yale, I wanted to let you know how proud I am of you. The measure of a man is not in what happens, but in how he chooses to <u>respond</u>. You have responded to getting fired by getting fired up! It's great to see you choosing to work out every day. It's great to see you choosing to read Alan Carr's book [to stop smoking]. It's great to see you working on your game and your Kickstarter campaign. Before your Kickstarter launches and you become a star, I wanted to take a moment to let you know how proud I am of you—no matter what happens with Kickstarter. Thanks for encouraging me to get moving and get a bike. I really enjoyed taking the inaugural ride with you today! Love, Mom*

I can now honestly say that I wouldn't have wanted him to miss out on the wisdom and maturity he gained by getting fired. It wasn't a terrible thing that he got fired—it was a great thing.

Update—on November 8, 2012, Yale's dream came true. His Kickstarter crowd funding campaign was successful, and he is now onto the next stage of becoming an entrepreneur and following his life-long passion of being a game designer. And it would not have happened if he hadn't been fired. So…getting fired turned out to be a blessing in disguise. Yale had a choice to become bitter or better, and he choose to become better.

"Money is eroding"

It can provide insight to consider your relationship with money by humanizing it. Is it a friend, a lover, a stranger, an enemy? Is it reliable, loyal, dependable? Or fickle, capricious, unreliable? Here's the essence of a recent coaching call with a recently-divorced client who was anxious and worried about money. I asked her, if money was a person, how would she feel about it?

Paula: I am frustrated at Money because it has been eroding since the divorce. I know that I am capable and competent! I know I am valuable. I am worried because Money is leaving me—just like my husband left me.

Aurora: What do you want Money to do?

Paula: Money should come to me easily and effortlessly. Money should show up when I need it. Money shouldn't wake me up with fear and anxiety in the middle of the night. Money should woo me like a lover and materialize whenever I need it, eager to do my bidding! I need Money to show up in greater abundance. I need Money to show up more frequently. I need Money to come from my clients, so I can be independent and feel good about my self-worth. I need Money to be reliable and dependable.

Aurora: What's the most painful thought you have about this issue?

Paula: Money is eroding.

Aurora: Would you like to do the Peace Method® on that thought?

Paula: Yes, please.

Aurora: Let's take a few deep breaths together and get centered in the present moment.

(brief meditation) Inhale and relax your body. Exhale and smile. Inhale coming fully into the present moment. Exhale knowing that it's a wonderful moment.

So… what's the present situation?

Paula: The present situation is that my net worth is eroding. I don't have a job and I'm spending $8,000 a month!

Aurora: What is the cost of believing this thought? How do you react when you believe the thought "money is eroding"?

Paula: I feel panic. I feel like a loser. I feel abandoned. I feel like a victim. I want to curl up and take a nap—not look for a job or start a business.

Aurora: Can you accept the thought "My money is eroding" without making war with it?

Paula: I don't know. I'll try.

Aurora: Can you accept that sometimes it is OK if your money is eroding? That life is like breathing—sometimes you inhale, sometimes you exhale. Sometimes it could be wise to allow your money to erode (for example to protect your health). It is just a snapshot in time. Other times, your money will not be eroding, it will be growing.

Paula: Yes, I can see that. I can accept that. That feels much more balanced and peaceful, thank you.

Aurora: What is there to appreciate about this situation? Or about the thought "my money is eroding"?

Paula: I could appreciate that if Steve had left me with a lot more money, I might not have to work—and I might end up spiraling into a depression. The thought "my money is eroding" is a call to action. I can appreciate that.

Aurora: What is the contrary of "My money is eroding"?

Paula: "My money is _not_ eroding."

Aurora: Tell me about that. How is that true?

Paula: Let me see…
     My money would not be eroding if I got a good job.
     I have $175,000 in savings and it is growing, some stocks increased in value, so that money is not eroding.
     I get $8,000/month in alimony, and I spend about the same, so really it is more like break-even.
     If I reduced my expenses, I could stop eroding my money. I could have time to go back to school and get more training, or start a business. I really don't have to panic. I have time to figure things out.
     If I increased my income, I could stop eroding my money. I have made good money in the past.

Aurora: So, given this exploration, what are you enthusiastic about now?

Paula: I'm enthusiastic about starting a business. I'm also enthusiastic about not being an ostrich and instead proactively looking at my situation and making the best of it. I'm enthusiastic about calling my former employer and seeing if they have an opening for me.

As you can see, as a result of this quick process, Paula was empowered to look at her finances more calmly and clearly. When she felt more peaceful, she was able to see opportunities to improve her situation.

"Money should show up when I need it"

In my experience, each painful thought is like a brick in a brick wall of a prison. On the other side of the prison is a beautiful garden with flowers and hummingbirds and a lake. Once one brick has been freed using the Peace Method®, you can see the garden. You can see freedom. You don't have to release every brick in the prison wall—you simply need a big enough hole to walk through to freedom. Patiently exploring adjacent bricks (painful thoughts) is the way to freedom.

On the same coaching call, we looked at another painful thought Paula had about money.

Paula: Money should show up when I need it.

Aurora: This assumes "Money <u>doesn't</u> show up when I need it." Can you see that?

Paula: Yes.

Aurora: Would you like to do the Peace Method® on the thought "Money doesn't show up when I need it"?

Paula: Yes.

Aurora: Take some deep breaths. Get centered in the present moment. Is this thought "Money <u>doesn't</u> show up when I need it" about the past, the present, or the future?

Paula: The present.

Aurora: What is the cost of this thought? How do you feel when you believe the thought "Money doesn't show up when I need it"?

Paula: I feel abandoned. I can't sleep at night. I worry that I'll end up a homeless bad lady. I feel like a failure. I'm too depressed to pick up the phone and call my former employer. I want to sleep all day.

Aurora: Every cloud has a silver lining, if you're willing to look for it. Are you willing?

Paula: Yes.

Aurora: What could there possibly be to appreciate?

Paula: I could appreciate that if money doesn't show up when I need it, then I need to go out and get it proactively. In other words, not to wait passively, but to act proactively. I could appreciate that.

Aurora: Could you accept that sometimes money shows up when you need it—and other times it doesn't? So make peace with the thought "Money doesn't show up when I need it" by accepting that sometimes that is true, and sometimes the opposite is true?

Paula: Yes, I can accept that. That feels much more peaceful, thanks.

Aurora: What's the contrary of "Money doesn't show up when I need it"?

Paula: "Money <u>does </u>show up when I need it."

Aurora: Tell me about that. How does money show up when you need it?

Paula: Let me see. Money <u>does</u> show up when I need it.

When my dog needed to go to the vet, I rented out the downstairs suite, so that was an example of money showing up when I needed it.

Ten years ago, when I really needed a job, I found a great job in just a few weeks, so money showed up when I needed it then.

When I needed to pay the mortgage two weeks ago, the alimony check showed up just in time to pay it.

Hmmm…so the truth is, money <u>does</u> show up when I need it! (she laughs)

Aurora: Good to notice! So, what are you enthusiastic about now?

Paula: I'm feeling enthusiastic about not panicking about money. Based upon my history, the evidence is that money <u>does</u> show up when I need it. I am enthusiastic about relaxing into trusting God to support me and our kids. It's going to be OK. I'm not going to become a bag lady!

Paula went from being stressed and anxious to laughing and being empowered in less than thirty minutes.

"Sally is keeping Brian from me"

Anna is frustrated by her son's new girlfriend's lack of poise and polish. Anna's son is in love with a girl that doesn't quite measure up to Anna's hopes for her son's future wife. Anna is eager to reconnect with her son (Brian), who has been away. The new girlfriend (Sally) is getting in the way. Anna volunteers to be coached on a group training call at the Grief Coach Academy.

Anna: Sally frustrates me because she butts in a lot. She's Brian's girlfriend. He brought her home with him from Seattle and she has a lot of uneducated opinions. She should think before speaking. Why is my son with her? Sally is not right for Brian.

Aurora: Are you upset because Sally is not right for Brian?

Anna: I guess it's more that I'd like more one-on-one time with my son. She's always around. It feels like Sally is keeping Brian from me. That's what is most upsetting.

Aurora: Would you be willing to do a demonstration of the Peace Method® with me on "Sally is keeping Brian from me"?

Anna: Absolutely, love to.

Aurora: Okay. So let's take a couple of deep, cleansing breaths and come fully in the present moment.

(after a brief meditation) Our bodies cannot tell the difference between a problem in our mind, or a problem in the present. So I'm curious. Is this thought "Sally is keeping Brian from me" primarily about the past, the future, or the present?

Anna: Most energy is about the future.

Aurora: Good to notice. We can never solve all potential future problems, but we can deal with the one challenge/opportunity (which means the same thing) that's right here, right now in the present moment.

I'm going to invite you to express your feelings. If you can't feel it, you can't heal it. So how do you feel with the thought "Sally is keeping Brian from me"?

Anna: Like a mamma bear.

Aurora: Tell me more about the mamma bear.

Anna: Well they would find the body, so that mamma bear is protective and ferocious.

Aurora: Okay. What else happens with the thought "Sally is keeping Brian from me"?

Anna: It makes me feel anxious and sad. I don't treat Brian as well as I could. I'm not as supportive. Maybe I'm a little more sharp with him and that hurts. That's not the legacy I want to leave from his visit.

Aurora: That's why I know that this is right process for you today sweetheart, because you're willing to be more conscious, and create a different legacy. So how do you treat Sally with the thought "Sally is keeping Brian from me"?

Anna: Well I cut her no slack. If she was on my boat she would be walking the plank, not a shadow of a doubt.

Aurora: All right. How do you treat yourself with the thought "Sally is keeping Brian from me"?

Anna: I don't like who I am.

Aurora: Ow! And how does that show up?

Anna: By not being as engaged, being more of a spectator.

Aurora: Whose business are you in mentally when you believe the thought "Sally is keeping Brian from me"?

Anna: God's business, even Brian's business and Sally's business.

Aurora: Okay, good to notice. And what happens when we are in other people's business—whether it's God's, Brian's or Sally's?

Anna: Not good, buttinsky.

Aurora: We always feel separate, anxious, disempowered. So does this thought "Sally is keeping Brian from me" bring peace or stress into your life?

Anna: Absolute 100% stress.

Aurora: Okay, good to notice. So imagine it's longer possible for you to believe the thought "Sally is keeping Brian from me." How would you be right now?

Anna: I'd be me, more calm. I'd like me again.

Aurora: That sounds good. Anything else you want to share around how you react when you believe this thought "Sally is keeping Brian from me" before we go onto the next step?

Anna: I get way too spicy.

Aurora: Spicy?

Anna: I give a zinger—and then I have regret. The fun of giving the zinger goes away really fast.

Aurora: That's beautiful wisdom coming from you. Awareness is everything because once you have awareness you can consciously choose something that would serve you better. So let's move onto the A of the Peace Method®, which is around accepting and appreciating. In my experience every cloud has a silver lining if you're willing to look for it.

Anna: Absolutely.

Aurora: So would you be willing to accept that in some moments over the next couple of days, that the truth may actually be "Sally is keeping Brian from me"? That may be true. Would you be willing to accept that without having to fight it or without attaching any particular meaning to it?

Just as you might look out the window and notice, "Oh, it's a rainy day." Okay, well I may need to change my plans or take my umbrella, but I don't need to resist it or deny it or fight it. You might think of some things you could do on a rainy day. And you know the weather will change. Everything changes. We know that for sure.

So would you be willing to accept "Sally is keeping Brian from me" and just notice it as useful information? Not as something that is attacking you or against you?

Anna: Absolutely I can look at it and accept it as a reality without the strings attached. So I can accept something that doesn't make me happy, yes.

Aurora: Would you be willing to accept it now?

Anna: Yes.

Aurora: Stress is caused by the war against what is. Does that make sense?

Anna: Yeah.

Aurora: So what is there to appreciate about the fact that Brian and Sally are both home visiting with you?

Anna: Well that they're here visiting.

Aurora: That's good.

Anna: And I appreciate that. She makes him smile.

Aurora: What can you appreciate about the fact that he chose to bring her?

Anna: That he has a companion for the times that I can't be with him and he has someone that he can connect with.

Aurora: That's a good thing. And some other young men choose to see their girlfriends instead of their mothers.

Anna: I'd have killed him, but yeah.

Aurora: So if this situation was actually a gift from your higher self how could it be a blessing?

Anna: The blessing is in the awareness for me that it's okay. He is his own person and I truly want him to be happy and that it's not—I like how you said that—it's not instead of. Not either/or but both/and. So there is a place for both of us. He chose to bring her into my life versus doing his own thing and not participating. That's a gift, the awareness.

Aurora: I love where you're going with that. How is this an opportunity to change a pattern that doesn't serve you?

Anna: Change a pattern that doesn't serve me? Hmmm…holding my tongue instead of having her hold hers. Their relationship will take its course. And choosing my battles, the ones that matter and letting the others go.

Aurora: That sounds like a whole bunch of wisdom. So let's consider the contrary. In my experience we suffer when we don't see the whole truth and all the possibilities. So would you be willing to consider some other possibilities?

Anna: Absolutely.

Aurora: What's a contrary of "Sally is keeping Brian from me"?

Anna: "Sally is not keeping Brian from me." Or "I am keeping Brian from me."

Aurora: Which one would you like to look at first?

Anna: "I'm keeping Brian from me."

Aurora: Tell me how that's so, that "you are keeping Brian from you"?

Anna: The only true power we have are the actions we take upon thoughts, not the thoughts themselves. So I can choose my reaction and where I want to vibrate whether it's acceptance, appreciation, or if I want to get spicy. When I get spicy, it's negative, so I'm actually pushing him away.

Aurora: Good to have that awareness. How else is "I am keeping Brian from me" true?

Anna: It's true because I'm not happily being myself. I'm not being proactive or offering suggestions of how we could spend our time together on this visit.

Aurora: So what we're learning from you is that "I am keeping Brian from me" is actually a true statement, at least some of the time. You are aware that your actions are only your only true power and that you can choose where you want to vibrate. You can choose if you show up peaceful or spicy. You are also noticing that "I am keeping Brian from me" is true because you're not showing up as fully present or as proactive about how the time might be spent together. So which is more true, "I am keeping Brian from me" or "Sally is keeping Brian from me"?

Anna: I'm keeping Brian from me.

Aurora: That's more true?

Anna: Absolutely.

Aurora: So how do you feel noticing that?

Anna: (laughs) Like I need a good talking to!

Aurora: (laughs) Well, you're getting one right now. So given this wisdom and this insight that you've had, what do you consciously choose? What are you enthusiastic about?

Anna: I'm enthusiastic about the thought that I can still be me and I don't have to have that hold me back. And I can still have that time that I want together because I'll find a way.

Aurora: That sounds like an action plan.

Anna: (happy) Yeah.

Aurora: Let's come back and look at the other contrary you mentioned, "Sally is not keeping Brian from me." How could that be true?

Anna: She can't hold a candle to me.

Aurora: Yeah, that's for sure. Moms are forever. Girlfriends come and go. How else is Sally not keeping Brian from you?

Anna: She's much more of a follower than a leader.

Aurora: You're a stronger leader, so if you express your natural leadership she'll tend to follow. Is that right?

Anna: Yes.

Aurora: Tell me one more way that "Sally is not keeping Brian from you" is true.

Anna: Just my feeling inside. I don't know how to put words to that.

Aurora: What is more true? "I am keeping Brian from me" or "Sally is keeping Brian from me"?

Anna: It's more true that "I am keeping Brian from me." I don't have to like her and she doesn't have to like me, but that's not the point. I can be more generous with allowing space for her.

Aurora: Okay. I'd like to look at one more contrary. I'm hearing in your voice a little flavor of sadness, and so I'd like to look at another angle. Let's explore "I am not keeping Brian from me." How is it true that you're not?

Anna: I've rearranged my schedule and provided a beautiful guest room for him and his girlfriend.

Aurora: Tell me more about "I'm not keeping Brian from me."

Anna: I have spent time with him. I have made suggestions, and we spent a wonderful day at the lake.

Aurora: Nice. Tell me more about "I'm not keeping Brian from me."

Anna: I'm allowing him to do the things that please him, to give him freedom. We don't have to be in the same proximity 24/7.

Aurora: And all of these things are going to keep him closer to you.

Anna: Yeah.

Aurora: So what I'm learning from you is "I'm not keeping Brian from me" is very true. He's there. He's visiting. You've rearranged your schedule. You've made a beautiful guest room. You've welcomed him as well as his girlfriend. You've spent time with him. You're allowing him to do his own thing. You had a fun time at the beach. So I'm hearing from you that "I'm not keeping Brian from me" is a true statement. Would you agree?

Anna: Yes.

Aurora: So what stands out to you from considering all of those possibilities? Which one of these seems to be most true?

Anna: The one that brings me the most peace is "I am not keeping Brian from me."

Aurora: Okay, and that's absolutely true because he's visiting. You have the proof.

Anna: Yeah.

Aurora: Great. So given all this wisdom that's come out of this process of exploring and looking at the deeper truths, what are you enthusiastic about now?

Anna: I'm enthusiastic to know that I do like myself and I'm not horrible.

Aurora: (laughs) I would agree! And what actions are you going to take you most wonderful, not horrible woman?

Anna: I am going to spend some time today with Sally and I'm going to be very, very pleasant because there is no reason not to be.

Aurora: And maybe now that you notice that the truth is that she is not keeping Brian from you, there might be an opening to discover something about her that you truly enjoy?

Anna: Yeah, that would be nice.

Aurora: And we can honor mamma bear because if you didn't have a mamma bear part of you the human species would not have survived. So anything else that you'd like to share about what you're enthusiastic about?

Anna: If this is the girlfriend that lasts, I have the opportunity to set a great foundation.

Aurora: How nice. And if it's not the girlfriend that lasts, you nonetheless will be setting a great foundation with your son.

Anna: Yes, either way.

Aurora: How were you feeling on a scale of one to ten when we began with one being bad, and ten being awesome around "Sally is keeping Brian from me"? And how do you feel now on the same scale of one to ten?

Anna: I was about a three or a four to start and now I'm like a nine.

Aurora: Big shift then.

Anna: Yeah, thank you Aurora.

Aurora: You're welcome. What stood out to you from this process?

Anna: That though I did the Peace Method® on myself and I know the steps that having someone else coach you through it is much more powerful because you have a witness, and because you didn't let it go. You were like a dog with a bone. I can let myself off the hook because sometimes for me it's easy enough to say well that's good enough when I feel empowered. But you picked up and you actually left me in a place of peace, which was a lot different than feeling empowered. It was calmer and when you took me to that next step, which was even deeper, that's where I found the real silver lining.

Aurora: Empowered is good, but peaceful and empowered is better. Good work, Anna.

I checked in with Anna a few months later. Anna shared that this coaching session improved that visit and helped her to take action to improve her relationship with her son's girlfriend. She was especially grateful because, as it turned out, Sally was not just a passing fling. Brian married her, so Sally became a member of the family, and Anna's daughter-in-law.

"I don't make enough money"

When you have a fearful thought, instead of running away from it, it can be very beneficial to do the opposite and lean into it. This fosters acceptance. The natural result of considering something all the way through is realizing that you can handle it. Often laughter arises as in this instance coaching Kathy, a student at the Grief Coach Academy.

In this coaching session, I focus Kathy's attention first on acceptance, releasing her fear with laughter, then we do the Peace Method® coaching process.

Kathy: I'm really fearful about money. I can't get ahead. I had myself in better shape. I had a 6 figure inheritance. I paid off my credit cards and we made a lump-sum payment against the mortgage on our home. We bought a house on 4.5 acres as our retirement home. I still have half of my inheritance, but now my credit cards are up again. I don't know where all the money went. I can't get ahead. I'm not making enough money.

Aurora: It sounds like you <u>do</u> know where the money went. You paid off your credit cards and paid down your mortgage. And you bought a retirement home on 4.5 acres.

Kathy: Right. And now we are going to refinance. We should be OK—there is a lot of equity in the home. We haven't refinanced since we bought it 7 years ago. But I just can't seem to get ahead. I don't make enough money.

Aurora: Would you be willing to "lean into" that instead of trying to fix or solve or avoid that for just a moment?

Kathy: Okay.

Aurora: So…you don't make enough money. So then what?

Kathy: I won't get my credit cards paid off.

Aurora: So then what?

Kathy: I feel fear. I won't have enough money.

Aurora: So then what?

Kathy: I won't be able to retire.

Aurora: So then what?

Kathy: I'll be working until I'm 90.

Aurora: So then what?

Kathy: We'll never live on our ranch full time.

Aurora: So then what?

Kathy: I'll die. (laughs)

Aurora: Could you handle all that?

Kathy: Yes, I could. I should stop saying "I'll be working until I'm 90." I say that all the time. I should cancel that.

Aurora: Yes, good idea. Would you be willing to do the Peace Method® on that thought "I don't make enough money"?

Kathy: Yes. Please.

Aurora: Let's take a few deep breaths. Get centered. Come fully into the present moment. Our bodies cannot tell the difference between a problem in our mind or a problem in the present moment. Get curious. Is this painful thought right here right now, in this present moment? Or are you in the past or the future?

Kathy: I'm not in the present. I'm in the future.

Aurora: Good to notice. We can never solve all potential future problems. It's important to express our feelings—and release them. What is the cost or consequence of believing this thought? How do you react when you believe the thought "I don't make enough money"?

Kathy: I feel that I'm not good enough. I feel that I'm not on the same level as others I come in contact with. I'm not living in a new house. I don't have a new car.

Aurora: When you notice other people have newer houses and cars, whose business are you in?

Kathy: I'm in other people's business.

Aurora: Okay, good to notice. When we are in other people's business we will always feel bad. When we bring our attention back to our own business, we are empowered.

Kathy: I can actually have pretty much everything I want.

Aurora: Good to notice! Any other reactions that you notice with the thought "I don't make enough money"?

Kathy: Stress! It feels like a vicious cycle.

Aurora: What can you possibly appreciate about the thought "I don't make enough money"?

Kathy: It helps me grow. It causes me to brainstorm new ideas. I'm motivated to explore and learn and grow. I'm on a path of self-improvement. I launched my jewelry business, I'm training and learning new skills. I've been networking and making new friends and contacts.

Aurora: Sounds like quite a bit to appreciate.

Kathy: Yes.

Aurora: Could you simply accept the thought "I don't make enough money" without it being painful? Sometimes that might be a fact. "I don't make enough money" could just be information. One month you might make enough money. Another month you might have an unexpected windfall—like your inheritance. And at another time "I don't make enough money" could be a fact, and helpful information so you can choose to earn more or spend less.

Kathy: Yes, without the thought "I'm not good enough" it doesn't have a charge.

Aurora: You're a wise woman. What's the contrary of "I don't make enough money"?

Kathy: I do make enough money.

Aurora: Tell me about that.

Kathy: Well, I make all my payments on everything I owe each month. I have a very good credit score. My house has been appraised to refinance. That will free up substantial money as we haven't refinanced in the 7 ½ years we've owned this house. I'm doing everything I want to do. I have enough money for my horses. Even if I had a lot more money, I wouldn't really do anything more.

Aurora: Sounds like you do make enough money. Is "I don't make enough money" even true?

Kathy: (laughs) No. I do make enough money.

Aurora: Good to know! All we need to be happy is to have something to be enthusiastic about. What are you enthusiastic about now, given this coaching?

Kathy: I'm enthusiastic about remembering that the truth is that I do make enough money, and remembering not to compare myself to others. I feel peaceful. Thanks.

Aurora: You're welcome.

When you're coaching, your job is done when your client laughs. Laughter signals a release of energy and a shift in awareness. More is accomplished through laughter than through tears.

"He cheated"

Fresh from learning that her son-in-law cheated on her daughter, Clare is shaken. She is understandably distraught, agitated, and angry. Family is very important to her. Clare is attending a Grief Coach Academy training event, and I invite her onto the stage to receive coaching support. After a brief meditation to get centered in the present moment, Clare expresses her feelings.

Clare: I am so mad at Peter, my son-in-law, because he has cheated on Teresa and has put our family in chaos. Peter shouldn't have cheated with another woman while he was out of town on business. Peter should be sorry for causing so many people so much pain. I need Peter to realize what he did has affected many people and has destroyed all respect I had for him.

Aurora: Let's see which one of these thoughts is the most painful. We want to look at one brick at a time. For example, "I need him to realize what he did" is separate from, "He affected many people" is separate from "He destroyed all the respect I had for him." What's the most painful thought?

Clare: I mean the root of this is that he cheated.

Aurora: Let's look at that then.

Clare: All right.

Aurora: Take a deep breath. So, "he cheated"—past, present, or future?

Clare: Probably the past, present. I would say it's past and it's present because it's just happened.

Aurora: So, past and present. Take a deep breath. It's good to notice that you can never change the past. You can only forgive it and let it go. The past doesn't change.

So how do you react when you believe the thought, "he cheated" — what happens?

Clare: I'm devastated because it causes so much heartache to all of us.

Aurora: Where does "devastated" show up in your body?

Clare: In my heart.

Aurora: I'm hearing some thoughts about other people being hurt also.

Clare: Right, because it doesn't affect just one of us, it affects all of us, and because of his selfishness and not thinking about his family.

Aurora: Okay. So, you have some other thoughts come up about him?

Clare: There are plenty of thoughts about him. Some I shouldn't say in public!

Aurora: All right. What else comes up for you, Clare, when you think the thought "he cheated"?

Clare: What was he thinking? Why did he not think about what he had at home? Why did he do it?

Aurora: Whose business are you in mentally?

Clare: Totally in his business, there's no doubt about it.

Aurora: How do we feel when we're in other people's business?

Clare: Very, very hard. It's not a good place to be.

Aurora: No. We're always disempowered because we're over there with Peter in his business. Leaving nobody here with you in your business. So how do you treat Peter, if only in your mind, when you think the thought "he cheated"?

Clare: I don't want to see him. I don't want to talk to him. I don't want to have anything to do with him.

Aurora: How do you treat Clare in your mind when you think the thought "he cheated"?

Clare: I think about how it's affecting so many other people not just me, but how it's affecting everyone.

Aurora: When you're thinking about that, whose business are you in?

Clare: I feel like it's mine, it's affecting my life.

Aurora: Right. But when you're thinking about all the other people whose lives it would be affecting?

Clare: I'm in their business, but I feel I need to protect.

Aurora: Right. When you're in many other people's business your energy is fractured into dozens of different places, leaving less and less here with Clare, where the point of power is. Does that make sense?

Clare: Yes.

Aurora: I'm not asking you to drop thought "he cheated" — but just put it in isolation for a moment. Take a deep breath. If it wasn't possible for you to believe the thought "he cheated" in this moment, how would you be?

Clare: I would be okay.

Aurora: It's good to notice that the cost of the thought "He cheated" is not being okay.

Clare: Right.

Aurora: Anything other feelings you'd like to express?

Clare: No, I think I did that already.

Aurora: So, would you be willing to allow the thought "he cheated" not as an attack but just as neutral and useful information?

Clare: That's pretty tough.

Aurora: It's tough but you're pretty tough, too.

Clare: Yes.

Aurora: Take a deep breath. When we resist "what is" it doesn't go away. When we allow "what is" we're empowered to make the wisest choice. Pain is part of life. Suffering is optional. Would you be willing to take a deep breath and look at this information "he cheated" — not as an attack on you or those that you love but kind of like "news flash information incoming to Clare"?

Clare: Yes, I could do that.

Aurora: Good. Would you do that?

Clare: I will do that.

Aurora: Would you do it now?

Clare: I will do it now.

Aurora: Take a deep breath. That is allowing. How does that feel?

Clare: Still shaky.

Aurora: Any better?

Clare: Yes.

Aurora: Good. Going in the right direction?

Clare: Definitely.

Aurora: That's what I like to hear.

Clare: Yes, going up.

Aurora: Going up, elevator going up, headed to the penthouse gradually. What is there that you could possibly appreciate about the thought or about the situation?

Clare: The only thing that I can think that I could appreciate is that Teresa would be happy, and anybody that has a child knows that you're only as happy as your child. For her to be happy would make me happy.

Aurora: I like where you're going. Tell me more about how you could appreciate Teresa's opportunity to be happy.

Clare: That she'd be in a better place and she could be the person that she really is without somebody else trying to make her something she's not.

Aurora: That sounds good. Let me ask you this, would you be willing to appreciate that he could've cheated and she wouldn't find out, and on the other hand, we have this situation where he cheated apparently and she does find out—which do you prefer? Do you prefer your daughter to know the truth or not?

Clare: Absolutely to know the truth.

Aurora: Yes. Could you appreciate that then?

Clare: Sure.

Aurora: Okay. That's good. Truth is good.

Clare: Truth is great.

Aurora: The truth shall set you free.

Clare: (smiling) That's what I've heard.

Aurora: Anything else you can appreciate about Teresa, your daughter?

Clare: That she's a great mom.

Aurora: About yourself?

Clare: That I'm there for her and the kids.

Aurora: Nice, sounds good. Take a deep breath. Bring in all that appreciation. Are you willing to consider the contrary? We suffer when we don't see the whole truth and all the possibilities.

Clare: Okay.

Aurora: So, what's the contrary of "he cheated"?

Clare: That he did <u>not</u> cheat.

Aurora: Okay. Tell me ways that that's true, "he did not cheat."

Clare: I don't have any. I don't know. I mean it's a fact.

Aurora: Tell me ways that "he did not cheat" is true. Does he cheat on his taxes?

Clare: No, not that I know of. That's his business.

Aurora: Tell me other ways he doesn't cheat. Does he cheat when you play cards with him?

Clare: I don't play cards with him.

Aurora: (teasing) Is that because he's a cheater?

Clare: Maybe, it could be. You know, I can't think of anything.

Aurora: So, every interaction you've ever had with this man, he's cheated every single time? Why would she have married him?

Clare: That's a good question. She married him, not me. Exactly.

Aurora: Well, see the problem with this whole thing is you're in other people's business, so you're not going to know. If your daughter was sitting here, it would be interesting to see what she might discover by looking at the contrary.

Clare: I'm the one in the seat.

Aurora: You're the one in the seat, right. Anything else you want to share about the contrary?

Clare: I don't think so.

Aurora: Looking at the contrary isn't very interesting when you're in other people's business, so let's move on. Given the wisdom that you've gotten so far, what are you enthusiastic about choosing now? What do you consciously choose?

Clare: I consciously choose to let him be in his business, and let my daughter and son-in-law take care of their marriage and their business.

Aurora: Right. That's much more peaceful.

Clare: It is.

Aurora: Good. You're looking calmer.

Clare: I feel much better.

Aurora: Good. How were you feeling on a scale of 1 to 10 at the beginning, and how are you feeling now?

Clare: I think it was pretty evident. I would say I was pretty far down there, I would say a two.

Aurora: And now?

Clare: Now, I'm thinking I'm probably like at a six.

Aurora: That's great.

Clare: Yes.

Aurora: Good progress. What brought you the most clarity?

Clare: That I need to get out of his business.

Aurora: Hallelujah. Let's give her a round of applause. Very nice work. From two to a six, that's huge. Thank you for being so coachable. A great coach is coachable, and you certainly are.

Clare: Thank you.

Aurora: Good work, honey. Anything else you want to share?

Clare: Just thank you for listening ladies and gentlemen. It has been a rough few days.

Aurora: Thanks for being here, Clare. You're in the right place. A the right time. Good job.

I'd like to point out a few things about this coaching example. When you are coaching someone who is raw with emotion, it is helpful to invite them to take a deep breath, as I did several times with Clare. This is calming and centering.

This is a "textbook" example of what happens when your coaching client is not dealing with something that belongs to them. The best coaching will help them realize that they are in someone else's business.

After the event, I called Clare to follow up. She cheerfully shared that the wisdom she gained from doing this process stayed with her, and gave her the calm and confidence she needed to help her husband deal with his anger. Realizing that this was their daughter's and son-in-law's business was the key to a peaceful and productive response. She was pleased to share that she and her husband were able to support their daughter and son-in-law by allowing them the space to work through their own problems, and decide whether to reconcile or divorce.

CONCLUSION

I trust this book has shown you how you can use the Peace Method® to release grief and stress rapidly. My experience is that this simple process provides insight, clarity, and grief relief in 30 minutes or less.

When you have a painful thought, write it down, and then take it through the five steps of the Peace Method®.

1. Take some deep breaths and come fully into the present moment. Is your stressful thought about the past, the present or the future? You can never change the past. You can never solve all potential future problems.
2. Fully express your thoughts and feelings. If you can't feel it, you can't heal it.
3. Accept the situation, your thoughts and your feelings. Resistance creates stress, not wisdom. What can you appreciate?
4. Consider the contrary. How could the opposite of your painful thought be true? How could this situation be a challenge calling forth your best?
5. What are you enthusiastic about being or doing now? Make a conscious choice and then take action.

You can benefit from doing this yourself as a daily journaling process.

GETTING A COACH FOR MORE SUPPORT

Journaling is great, but there's nothing like having the support of a coach to personally support you through life's challenges, and help you get clear on a vision for the future that fills you with enthusiasm.

When you are dealing with major life challenges, having a coach is not simply nice to have, it is a necessary strategy. Do yourself a favor and get coaching so that you can create the life you desire more quickly and easily.

With the support of a certified From Heartbreak to Happiness® coach, people can release grief rapidly, following a proven system. The Peace Method® is one step of a nine-step coaching recipe designed to help you go From Heartbreak to Happiness®. Coaching is the fast and easy way to reclaim peace of mind.

Having your own personal coach gives you one-on-one personal support and feedback. No one can see their own blind spots. Your coach will talk you through other coaching processes in a specific coaching recipe. Coaching is typically done over the phone in 30 minute sessions.

Unresolved grief is an epidemic. Death, divorce, disease, job loss, bankruptcy, having a child with special needs, or a parent with Alzheimers—leave a wake of grief. Unresolved grief can accelerate aging, suppress the immune system, and depress productivity and income. It can cause premature aging of up to a decade. Grief can even trigger death.

In contrast, happy people live 7 years longer, are 35% less likely to get sick and earn a million dollars more over their lifetime, according to one study. Transcending grief can lead to deep wisdom, insight, and discovering your life's purpose.

The coaches I train at the Grief Coach Academy are shining examples of discovering the gifts in their own personal grief, alchemizing that lead into gold, transmuting it and transforming it, and then powerfully helping others.

BECOMING A COACH

This book gives you a taste for how you could use the Peace Method® as a coaching tool. At the Grief Coach Academy, we train coaches to master the coaching skills necessary to help their clients through grief or heartbreak. The Peace Method® is just one of many powerful coaching processes that you will learn.

You can find out more about becoming a certified coach here: www.GriefCoachAcademy.com.

In order to be a great coach, you will need practice and in-depth training, which is beyond the scope of what a book can provide. Your clients deserve excellent coaching, so do yourself and your clients a favor — invest in getting the proper training.

My vision is to change how people think about and recover from grief. To achieve that, I have created a systematic recipe of coaching tools and a comprehensive study program that includes videos, audios, and training manuals in a convenient home-study coach training program, as well as a VIP program with live events and one-on-one coaching and mentoring.

My dream is to get this training program into every church, every hospital, every hospice, every nursing school, every Fortune 500 human resources department, and every other place it can help people who help grieving people. If you'd like to be part of this vision, we'd love to have you join us.

Having great coaching and communication skills is essential to helping yourself and helping others. Learn more coaching skills today. Get a series of free coach training videos here: www.GetCoachTraining.com.

ABOUT THE AUTHOR

Aurora Winter

Formerly a film and TV executive producer, Aurora Winter is America's leading expert at empowering people to go From Heartbreak to Happiness®. Aurora is the Founder of the Grief Coach Academy, which is the first coach training school devoted exclusively to training coaches how to coach their clients through grief and From Heartbreak to Happiness®.

Millions of people suffer from grief for years. Aurora's vision is to change how rapidly people recover from grief. Together with the team of coaches she is training at the Grief Coach Academy, she is doing just that.

A popular guest on TV and radio, Aurora has been featured on ABC-TV, CBS-TV, Fox-TV, Oprah radio and more. She has reached over a million people with her message of hope, healing, and happiness.

Aurora is the author of *From Heartbreak to Happiness, Encouraging Words,* and *Grief Relief in 30 Minutes* as well as many audio and video training programs, audio books, and other resources to help people become happier more rapidly and easily.

RESOURCES AT A GLANCE

Get your bonuses! Visit:

www.GetCoachTraining.com
Get 5 free coach training videos—learn coaching tools to help yourself and help others. You will learn bonus coaching skills that are not covered in this book.

Learn what to say—and not say—to encourage others. Learn how to see at a glance if your life is off-balance—and what to do about it. Learn how to double your happiness and peaceful productivity. Learn the 5 secrets of successful coaches, and more!
(Over $100 value—yours free for a limited time.)

www.AuroraWinter.com
Get Aurora to speak at your next event. Serious inquires only, please: 866-344-3108 or Aurora@AuroraWinter.com

www.GriefCoachAcademy.com
Interested in a career helping others? Learn how you can make a difference. Find out about our upcoming teleseminars and events. Books, audio books, CDs, home study training, articles, TV interviews, and more resources online.

16763231R00131

Made in the USA
Charleston, SC
09 January 2013